RUN,
The Story of Sam and Rachel Boymel

Sam Boymel

Rachel Boymel

RUN, MY CHILD

The Story of Sam and Rachel Boymel

Yad Vashem ✶ Jerusalem
The International Institute for Holocaust Research

Run, My Child
The Story of Sam and Rachel Boymel

Conducted and written by Docostory Ltd.

Academic Editor: Tikva Fatal-Cnaani
Language Editor: Judith Appleton
Managing Editor: Leah Goldstein

© 2010 All rights of the English edition are reserved to Yad Vashem
P.O. Box 3477, Jerusalem 91034, Israel
publications.marketing@yadvashem.org.il

ISBN 978-965-308-364-6

Typesetting: Judith Sternberg
Produced by: Printiv Press

Printed in Israel

In deep appreciation to Shraga I. Mekel, Development Director of the American Society for Yad Vashem, who initiated the writing of this book and conducted the preliminary interviews with Sam and Rachel Boymel. Our thanks also extend to Sharon Guttman Marcus, who edited the initial material.

TABLE OF CONTENTS

PART 1: EUROPE

My mother's words – Where I came from – The Tzaddik and the
Chief of Police – The *"Kaddish"* – All for her children – Apples
and stitches – Kosher and *treif* – Shabbes and Passover – All for
our mother – Happy, despite it all

In my dream – The horse in the garden – Holding hands in the
park – My mother's kitchen – Watching over me – The girl in
the *cheder* – Holidays in Ozierany – Dreams fly away

Ribbentrop-Molotov – Working for the Russians – "Yevrei, run
away!" – The Germans crash the party – Dawn of the ghetto –
Slaves of the German war machine – Hunger and fear – The brick
factory – What I saw – A mother's love

This is Russia now – The Promised Land – Kept in the
dark – Out of the clear blue sky – Nowhere to run – A girl in the
ghetto – Under the bed, behind locked doors – The ghetto's end

PART II: AMERICA

"If you want your husband to live" – The auction – Garden Manor
– 100% of the business – The inspector – Eight times eight –
Into the bank – My mother's voice – We never talked about it
– The "Bonds" – Turzysk – The bones in the *shtetl*

PART III: AFTERWORD

PART I: EUROPE

SAM, BEFORE THE WAR

My mother's words

"Run, my child! Run!"

My mother's last words still echo in my mind. They reverberate clearly over a chasm of sixty years. When I retell my story, I often start with that fateful day when my family lost their lives and I was born into another existence – one of hiding and running, hunger and fear, survival at all costs. It is as if my life began at that precise moment, and nothing before it existed.

"If you live through the war, don't forget where you came from!" my mother cried out to me. I was too young and terrified then to understand her parting words, but I have had a lifetime to reflect on her wisdom. I owe my life to my mother. She taught me the importance of giving and remembrance. I have shared my story many times before, but never as completely as I mean to do within this book. The story of my childhood, my family and my hometown are as important as the horrors of the Holocaust, for it is the story of all that was lost. And that is where I shall begin.

Where I came from

I was born in Turzysk, Poland (today Turijsk, Ukraine), on May 5, 1925. My American passport and driver's license would argue that I was, in fact, born two years earlier, in 1923. Though this mistake was simply due to a mix-up at the immigration office, a misunderstanding due to my utter lack of English at the time, there was some truth to be found in it. I often felt older than my age, as we were all forced to grow up too fast.

In those days, women gave birth at home with a midwife; there was no hospital and there were no doctors. I came into the world in this manner, born to my parents Rochel and Zelig Bojmel and to the thriving Jewish community of Turzysk.

The first Jews had arrived in Turzysk in the 16th century, but the ancient city dated back to the end of the 11th century, when it was established in Volhynia Province of Ukraine. In 1319, it was conquered by the Lithuanians and in 1365 was ceded to the King of Poland, Kazimierz the Great. Later it would be returned to Russia, and finally, after World War I, Turzysk became part of Poland.

The Jewish population grew more and more prominent between the 18th and early 20th centuries. The town became somewhat renowned due to a local well-educated Jewish physician, Dr. Moshe Markuza. He was very popular among Jews and non-Jews, and had good relations with the authorities and nobility in the region. Their support enabled him to produce a medical handbook written in the Yiddish language, in Hebrew letters, to be used by the poor. Published in 1770, this was the only medical handbook ever written in the Yiddish language.

The Turzysk where I grew up is long gone. It lives on only in the memories of its few survivors, me included. The town had a Hebrew library with thousands of books, and a Yiddish school with its own large library. Jewish culture and social life prospered in Turzysk, with Jewish educational institutions developing freely, as well as political parties, law courts, drama clubs, lecturers, dances, artworks and photography. Turzysk was renowned for its Yiddish theater and boasted several drama circles, amongst them the Zionist Drama Circle led by Avraham Silver and the "*Baal Meloches*" [Tradesmen] Drama Circle. Turzysk was also the home of three famous poets and writers: the Ulitzki Brothers, Zishe Weinper and Arie Tabkal.

The Turia River separated the suburb and the town, which was mostly populated by Jews. There were around 1,200 Jews in Turzysk on the eve of the Second World War; the Ukrainians were a minority. In the spring and fall, the waters of the river rose and created rivulets. These were used by the women for washing clothes. The Turia River was deep enough to allow boating. It was common to hear frogs making their melodious sounds during spring and summer evenings, and wild geese could often be seen above the river. On an island in the center of the Turia River the ruins of an ancient fortress towered over the *shtetl* [Jewish townlet] and became a meeting spot for lovers. In the center of town was the city's market. There was a row of four stores on one corner on one side of the street, with the Catholic Church on the other corner, and next to it the Russian Orthodox Church.

As a consequence of Jewish oppression under Russian rule, various ideological movements developed that were embraced by the Jews of Turzysk. The Zionism movement was in full bloom. A new Zionist Youth Organization, *Hashomer HaTzair*, trained its members to defend themselves against Ukrainian pogroms and to be ready to emigrate to Mandatory Palestine. Other youth movements such as *Beitar*, a conservative or rightist group that advocated the creation of a Jewish state, enjoyed support in Turzysk. Youngsters belonged to these various groups, and their differences manifested themselves in healthy competitions on the soccer field.

My family followed the Bund Movement, a left-wing Jewish socialist political movement founded in Vilnius in 1897 by a small group of workers and intellectuals. This movement strove to abolish discrimination against Jews and reconstitute Russia. The Bund movement was the most effective socialist organization in the country, and was active in Poland between the wars. As a member of the Bund, I attended their school, where I learned Yiddish. Afterwards I attended *Cheder* [a Jewish religious preschool], a room in which boys from about five years old studied Hebrew and the Torah.

The Tzaddik and the Chief of Police

Turzysk was also well-known in the Hasidic world, due to "The Maggid from Turzysk" (1770–1837). The term "*maggid*" had two special connotations: a popular and often itinerant preacher, as well as an angel or super-spirit that conveyed teachings to scholars worthy of such communication in mysterious ways. The Maggid from Turzysk was a typical, well-respected and influential itinerant preacher who spoke wherever Jewish leaders, as well as large masses of the people, gathered. There he expressed himself quite freely, covering the shortcomings of the rabbis as well as of the laity, undeterred by any consideration of fear.

On the 20th day of the Hebrew month of Tammuz, the anniversary of the Maggid's death, thousands of Hasidim and *Admorim* [grand rabbis] from Poland gathered in Turzysk. Every year, on the night of the Maggid's *Yahrzeit* [anniversary of death] hundreds of Jews labored at desks set up in the main street, writing "*Kvitlach*" [notes] for themselves and those who didn't know how to read and write. The next day everybody would come to the holy "*ohel*" [burial tent] and slide their notes into its notches and cracks, hoping that the Maggid, who was also known as the *Tzaddik* [righteous person], would hear their request and intercede with God on their behalf.

It was as if our town had its very own "Wailing Wall." If you couldn't have a baby, or if you couldn't make a living, it would be written on a note and put in the *ohel*. There were no doctors to take care of your health; only your faith in the Tzaddik. The power of the Maggid of Turzysk was so renowned that the non-Jewish Polish chief of police, a terrible man, came over to the rabbis and said, "My wife can't have a baby." In the interest of keeping the Poles and the Germans happy, the chief's command was obeyed and a note was written and thrown in on his behalf. Exactly nine months later, his wife gave birth to a baby boy, proof of the gravesite's mystical powers.

As a result, when the Germans would later try to make life difficult for the Jews of Turzysk, the police chief used all his powers to temper matters. He would turn a blind eye when he observed youngsters leaving the ghetto for food. If at all possible, he used his office to protect the Jews. To this day, the grave still lays undisturbed in the middle of the city. The Germans didn't dare touch it, for fear of retribution.

The "Kaddish"

My father Zelig was originally from Masiv, a town about twenty miles from Turzysk. I recall hazy summers spent in Masiv with my aunts, Father's sisters, whose names are lost to me now. They were the only family I had on my father's side. I never had the chance to meet my paternal grandparents. My mother would take me over to spend time with my aunts as a holiday treat. My parents were quite poor, and these two aunts of mine were well off. The sisters took care of me; they fed me well and bought me a pair of pants or a new shirt for Rosh Hashanah.

Zelig was a cobbler. He had a little shop, and people came by when they needed their shoes mended. Nobody could afford to buy new shoes, and he himself barely made any money, just a few zlotys for food. His customers at the time were both Jews and Gentiles. He spoke Yiddish, Polish and Ukrainian. He was a religious man, though not Hassidic, and he put on *tefillin* [phylacteries] every morning. He did not stand out: he was a short man, always dressed in ordinary clothes.

I had three sisters. Chasia, the eldest, was born in 1922. Second was Reisel. Five years after I was born, my parents had another daughter, my little sister Malka. My father was a very sick man; he suffered from an illness of the lungs, most likely tuberculosis. When Malka was still a small baby, Zelig fell ill. His sisters, having more money than we, insisted he be put under their care. They checked him into a hospital in Masiv. It was the last time my mother ever saw her husband.

He died away from his family. Word came back that the Polish hospital staff was openly antisemitic, and would not do anything for my father. As a child, I overheard pain-stricken discussions about how they had poisoned him to death. I will never know the details of my father's last days. If he was not poisoned, then he was simply allowed to die. He was buried in Masiv by his sisters. My mother could not even attend her husband's funeral.

My father's death transformed me. I had a new, cherished place within the family; I was now "the *Kaddish*," the only son capable of saying the Kaddish prayer of mourning for the dead. For the Jewish family, "the Kaddish" was God. As a five-year-old child, my mother took me to the big synagogue in Turzysk morning and night. I was placed in a chair and prompted to say the Kaddish for my late father. When my sisters and I got a piece of bread or two for lunch, mine was the only one that had been spread with marmalade, for I was "the Kaddish."

All for her children

My mother Rochel was born and raised in Turzysk. Her maiden name was Opeliner. She was a proud woman, who bore the hardships life dealt her with great dignity. She never asked for a handout. She was a poor widow, left to take care of four children, but she never uttered a word of complaint, never questioned God or broke down in self-pity.

After my father's death, my maternal grandparents took us in. My grandfather Mort Hirsh Opeliner and my grandmother Bassia Opeliner lived in Turzysk with a few of their children who had not yet married. My mother was one of ten children: seven daughters and three sons. Now that tragedy had rejoined Rochel with her unmarried siblings, Bassia allotted one room for her and her orphaned family. It was a little room with only two mattresses on the floor. My mother and I shared one, and my three sisters shared the other. There was no running water in the house.

My mother worked to support us. She ran around washing clothes and cleaning the houses of the wealthier Jewish families in the area for a pittance. On Fridays, I used to pump water from the street and carry the overflowing buckets for her, so that she could wash people's clothes. She was too weak to lug the heavy buckets up to the homes on the second floors. I was six or seven years old at the time, and already shaping up to be a strong young boy.

The people my mother worked for treated her terribly. They were Jewish, and she was a Jewish widow fallen on hard times, but if they found a Gentile worker who could do their housework for a few pennies less they didn't hesitate before throwing my mother out on the street. At times when I glanced at my mother I caught her crying, but she never said a word about it. Her thoughts were with her family, not her own troubles. My mother used to take me by the hand to school and wait outside to pick me up so that nobody would touch me. She protected me because I had no father. I knew then that my mother would give her life for me.

Apples and stitches

Though she took us in, my grandmother offered no additional help. When it came to food or clothes, my mother was still on her own. As a little boy, I worked for my grandmother like a dog. She had a bakery and was very well off. She bought apples and cherries and all kinds of fruits from the Ukrainian farmers and then held a private market in her shop, where she sold the fresh produce. She couldn't read or write, but she was a businesswoman. She used to take me away from my mother and put me in the basement, where I was to sort the apples and remove the rotten ones. I received nothing in return for this work, but it was only natural that I, just a child, should steal some apples for myself, and that was just what I did.

My grandfather ran a tailor's shop with one of his sons. I was put to work there as well, and I used to help my grandfather by spending hours taking out stitches. The work was done without the help of any machines back then. Unlike my grandmother, he used to reward me with a couple of pennies for the work.

Kosher and "treif"

I went to the *mikveh* with my grandfather on Friday afternoons. This is the ritual bath in which Orthodox men immerse themselves before each Sabbath – the "Shabbes." We'd close up the shop on Friday and head off to the *mikveh*. He would hold my hand as we walked. The *mikveh* was always full of people. There was no soap and there were no towels; instead I would slap my grandfather with tree branches as a means of cleansing his body. Not only were we performing a mitzvah by taking part in this holy act, but at the same time, since we didn't have a bathtub at home, we were able to bathe and clean ourselves as well.

My grandfather Mort had been to America a few times before my birth. His plan was to go over there, make money and eventually bring the whole family over to join him. But he was a very religious man who wouldn't work on Shabbes and wouldn't touch his lips to anything that wasn't kosher. America was simply unfit in his eyes. Several years later on, when our *shtetl* had become a ghetto, we argued with him.

"Zeideh!" we screamed. "You were in America so many times. Why did you come back?"

He replied, "America is *treife* [unkosher]." "The streets of America are '*treife*,' and they should burn!" An observant Jew, he had watched Americans driving their cars on the Sabbath and shuddered. America was not a "kosher" enough place to live.

Shabbes and Passover

Women of poorer families used to roam the streets and dirt roads of the *shtetl* asking the richer women for challah [traditional plaited bread] for their Shabbes dinner. My mother didn't want handouts. Another option was to pawn pillows: if you wanted challah for Friday night and you didn't have the money for it, you gave away your pillows until you could afford to buy them back. Every so often, my mother would do this. When possible, she would also buy a chicken and prepare a soup. We would all eat together, but my mother would never touch the chicken. She said she couldn't eat, and gave everything to us. We regarded those Fridays as a feast.

In the adjacent room, my grandparents and aunts and uncles would also have their Friday night meal. My grandfather would call me to sit with him, but they never offered me any food. When I returned to our little room, my mother asked me, "They didn't give you anything to eat, my child?" and I would answer, "No."

On the eve of Passover, American Jews used to send 'mashchiten' – 'gmilut hassidim' [charity] – to the poverty-stricken Jews in Europe. They'd go to their rabbi, sell their hametz [leavened foods that are forbidden on Passover] and give the money to those less fortunate. There were people from Turzysk in New York, and their charity money was sent back to the Jewish community in my hometown to buy matzos. Each poor family received five dollars.

My mother would anxiously await these five dollars. As Passover grew near, she took on more floors to wash and did as much work as she could bear. Her extra earnings were used for buying potatoes and the ingredients for red borscht. The five dollars bought us the matzos. We'd buy the broken matzos because they were cheaper. My mother never passed up having a chicken for our Passover meal. On the holiday night, I joined my grandparents' seder in the other room. As the youngest boy, I sang the 'ma nishtana' questions, asking, "Why is this night different from other nights?" and once I had performed my duty, I was sent over to my own family in our little room, and that was it. I was never angry at my grandparents. I didn't know any better and thought that was the way things were.

All for our mother

As I grew older, I began to take on more work for my mother's benefit. I was put to work for one of my uncles, my mother's brother Yoileh. He had a pair of horses and a wagon, which he used as a cab that shuttled people to and from the nearby city of Kowel. I'd sit with the horse, ride to Kowel and bring a new group of passengers with me on the way back. I was a boy of no more than seven and Kowel was a big city, but I knew where to go. The wagon carried about twenty passengers per trip, and I rode it back and forth several times a day. In this way, I got a taste of the big world that lay outside of Turzysk.

Yoileh used to buy pigeons for me. I owned many pigeons thanks to my uncle's kindness. A few of the pigeons became our meals; we took them to a *shochet* [ritual slaughterer] and cooked them up. The others I sold as carrier pigeons for the mail. My Uncle Yoileh taught me all about the use of pigeons as mail carriers. Back then this was a common way of delivering your mail to its destination in a speedy manner. The pigeons provided me with a bit of additional income. In addition to the pigeons, Yoileh would give me a few pennies now and then. He was unmarried and had no children, and he took a liking to me, his nephew. He was very nice to me. At some point he became our sixth roommate. His mother, my grandmother, put a bed in our room, and he slept with us.

I had another uncle on my mother's side whose name was Leibel. Married with three or four children, he did not share my grandmother's house but had his own in town. Whenever people built a new house in Turzysk or in the neighboring villages, they came to Leibel to have their windows and doors installed. He was very well-known by both Jews and Gentiles. He was a fine carpenter, and he taught me the craft at a very young age.

I had learned a little bit of carpentry by observing a local man in his woodshop. This man took me in to teach me how to be a carpenter. He felt sorry for me and said he would teach me, but in fact he did nothing for me. At times he gave me a little something to eat, but he never paid me for the work I did. When the workday was over, he'd close up shop and have me come over to his house and clean it. Though I got no payment out of it, I gained experience. My hands were my tools.

On the days when Leibel took me out with him, my mother would dress me up to look older than my age. Leibel and I would go into the village of Rastov (Rastiv) and knock on the doors of the non-Jewish townsmen, asking if they needed us to do any repair work. We did work other than carpentry if necessary; people gave us pots that had holes in them, and we repaired the holes. I was just a kid, and I didn't know any of the customers, but Leibel was well-acquainted with them all. One of his frequent customers was a Jewish girl who had married a Gentile Polish man. The synagogue had excommunicated her, but we figured that since she was still Jewish, she might take us in and give us work.

My sisters finished elementary school and then learned how to be seamstresses because my mother needed more money. They were twelve or thirteen years old at the time. They learned how to sew in a small shop in the *shtetl*, much like I learned my trades. They learned everything by hand, since nobody had a sewing machine back then. All the money they and I made went to my mother. We had no need for it. My mother used the money to take care of us and buy us food and clothes.

Happy, despite it all

The atmosphere in the *shtetl* was very nice. We got along with the non-Jews. We used to have a "*Shabbes Goy*" ["Sabbath Gentile"] who came over during the Sabbath to light the fire for us, since we were not permitted to light a fire on the Sabbath. We did not go to the same school as the non-Jews, but I knew our *Shabbes Goy* and we were very close when we were kids. We played soccer together. I was good at sports, but my mother wouldn't let me play. She was afraid someone would hit me. I always listened to my mother. I didn't have a father; she was all I had.

The Turia River froze during the cold winters. We warmed our small room with wood. If you had dry wood, that meant you were rich. The poor got the bad, wet pieces of wood. It was very difficult to get them to burn, and even when you succeeded they didn't burn very well. But we got by. We didn't know any other way of life. When we huddled around the fire I felt close to my family. It didn't even matter whether the fire burned or not, because being with them filled me with such warmth I knew I would be all right as long we had each other.

This was a joyful time for us. There was always laughter, and we were together. Life may not have been easy, but we were very happy. We didn't know our lives were poor. My mother always hugged me and kissed me. I got a lot of love from her. You couldn't find a mother like her anywhere in the world...

RACHEL, BEFORE THE WAR

In my dream

When I was just a little girl, I often woke from dreams so vivid they seemed indistinguishable from reality. In one of these dreams, a great bomb had destroyed humanity. I walked endlessly across a nightmarish landscape, unable to find a single living soul. Everybody had disappeared. An overwhelming wave of death and loneliness washed over me and woke me. I cried in my bed. My mother hurried to my side and asked me what was wrong. I began to recount my vision, but she had heard enough. "Go to sleep, my child," she said. She comforted me, "It's only a dream."

This dream came to me before I knew anything of the Germans, Hitler or the bomb, long before its nightmarish landscape became a reality for me. Yet I survived and was able to make better, brighter dreams come true in my life. Today I carry both the nightmares and the blessings with me. To ignore one or the other is to tell half the story. In this book, I wish to share everything: all that I've gained and all that I've lost. My story begins with the love of my parents...

The horse in the garden

My mother told the story of how she and my father met to anybody who would listen, and I was always happy to hear it. The year was 1918. The Russian civil war had been going on for many months. My father, Yankel Czerkiewicz, was enlisted in the army at the time. During a holiday leave he happened to stop by in Ozierany (today Ozerany), the little Polish town where my mother lived and the same town that would one day become my birthplace (there were about 1,000 Jews living in Ozierany between the two World Wars). At the time, the most popular mode of transportation was by horseback. Yankel came upon a beautiful garden and chose a particular tree within it to tie his horse.

My mother noticed the young man in uniform tying his horse to a tree, and came out to speak to him. It was customary in those days for all the Jewish soldiers to ride into the small towns for the holidays and have kosher food cooked for them by the locals, but my mother offered him no such thing. Instead, she asked him, nicely and politely, if he could remove his horse from her family's garden. My father took one look at her and knew he would never find a prettier woman. For Yankel, this was love at first sight.

Her name was Pessa Fruma Belfer, and she was indeed very beautiful. She had long black hair and gorgeous eyes. Though she had offered no invitation, my father pursued her from that moment on. He came to the Belfer household every chance he had and talked to my grandfather, Yossel Belfer. My mother wasn't impressed. She was beautiful, and had many suitors. But Yankel wouldn't let go until my grandfather agreed, and Pessa Fruma was soon to follow.

She finally fell in love with her relentless suitor and married him at the young age of eighteen. Yankel's dream had come true. He took her to Warsaw to meet his parents and his brothers. The ceremony was held in my hometown.

Holding hands in the park

My parents' first child was a boy, who passed away shortly after his *bris* [ritual circumcision]. Sadly, infant deaths were more frequent in those days. My parents recovered and had my older brother Meyer in 1922. I was born on January 1, 1925, their second child and only girl out of five. I was named after my grandmother Rochel on my mother's side, who had already passed away. I had three younger brothers: Zalman, Menachem and Yossel. My maternal grandfather had already died by the time my youngest brother was born, and so Yossel was named after him. This was in 1935, and at ten years old, I was old enough to clearly remember the joy of Yossel's *bris*.

We lived in a big house that had been divided in two for two families. My mother's brother, Uncle Mendel, lived in the other half with his family. During my childhood, income was, thankfully, never a problem, and we had plenty of food. It was such a pretty home and so cozy inside. My mother kept it immaculate with the help of a Ukrainian woman, a non-Jew, who lived with us. There was no running water in our house, yet everybody was so clean you wouldn't know from looking at us that we drew our water from the well outside. The toilet was outside as well, and kept just as clean. Ever since I can remember, I knew how to behave and how to clean by myself. This was how our mother brought us up. On Fridays, she had all of us children pitch in as well; we would make our home spotless, and then she would dress us and send us out to the park. We went out holding hands, all five of us. We were a happy family.

My mother's kitchen

My mother was a wonderful cook. Whatever she prepared – whether it was chicken or gefilte fish or any other dish – came out tasting like no one else's. Her cooking was loved by everyone in the family. Her sister's children, my cousins Michael and Betzalel

Bernstein, used to tell me, "When your mother cooked a potato, nobody thought they were eating potatoes. It was something else."

My mother would also bake an assortment of wonderful pastries, including a sweet challah, for our Friday nights and holidays. I used to watch her from just outside the kitchen. I had a head of flowing hair, and my mother didn't want me to cover it with a scarf; she thought I looked beautiful as I was. But it was because of my hair that she didn't let me near the kitchen while she was baking. Her kitchen was spotless. If my hands were clean, sometimes she would give me a piece of dough to play with. Those were some of my happiest childhood memories.

In the winter time we had a family tradition of eating breakfast in bed. My mother made the chocolate milk herself, which she served it with cheese pretzels or *latkes* [pancakes] from sour milk or potatoes, whatever she had felt like baking. Food had to be prepared and then eaten, because we had no refrigerator. Everything we ate was freshly cooked or baked. When I think of my mother, I think of the wonderful aromas that wafted out of her kitchen.

When I think of my father, cigarette smoke comes to mind. He was a heavy smoker, yet he wouldn't touch a cigarette on Shabbat or on the holidays. He had another habit: my mother's cookies. As a little girl, I remember her getting up at 2 a.m. and starting to bake. When she did so, the first thing she baked was always cookies for her husband. He'd wake up at odd hours of the night and eat them. I knew this because I could hear the sounds of him eating her cookies coming from the kitchen on those nights when I woke up and had to go to the toilet. Those sounds always brought a smile to my face.

Watching over me

My father Yankel was a salesman. He would travel to Warsaw and buy merchandise, primarily ladies' suits, and then go out to the nearby villages and sell his stock. The farmers out there had no opportunity to go out and buy things for themselves; they depended on someone like my father to come to them. Some paid him with money; others offered goods in exchange. My father was paid with sheep and calves and all that can be found on a farm.

Other than stocking up on his merchandise, my father took advantage of his business trips to Warsaw and bought gifts for us all. He brought me the most beautiful toys, so wonderful that they stick in my mind even after all these years. He even brought me a little sewing machine. I wanted to keep everything that he brought me. Before one of the holidays, he brought me a pair of shoes that were a little small on me, but I insisted on wearing them no matter what.

Since boys would not play with girls' toys, whenever I wanted to play with my new gifts I had to go over to my cousins, who were girls. I'd often return from these play dates with things missing. They used to take my toys away from me. My mother would hide in the trees and watch over us; there were plenty of trees to hide behind in our town. I was unaware of her watching over me. It was only later on that she told me that she'd been there, in the trees, nearly every time I'd gone over to play.

My first earrings were a gift from my father. My mother was very conscious of who took my toys, and when I went over glowing with joy over my new diamond earrings, only to return home without them, she had seen it happen. She held her tongue because they were family. Shortly after that, my father went on another trip to Warsaw. This was his livelihood, and he used to go very often. He returned with another pair of earrings for me. This time around, when a woman came over and admired my earrings, my mother appeared out of the trees, out of nowhere as far as I was concerned, and said, "Oh, not this time. This time, I'm watching."

The girl in the cheder

I came from a very religious family. My grandfather Yossel on my mother's side was a rabbi. During my early childhood my grandfather lived with us. I remember being as young as two-and-a-half years old and seeing his many students coming over to the house where he taught them Gemara and Mishnah. He was well-respected in the Ozierany synagogue, which was not far from our house. We could walk there.

Because my grandfather was such a beloved rabbi, I wasn't sent to kindergarten. Instead I was sent to *Cheder* from the age of two, which is what religious Jews did. I wore socks up to my knees and a skirt. My mother didn't wear a *sheitel*, a wig that orthodox women would wear; instead she wore a nice little scarf to cover her hair. Despite her appearance, she was very religious in her heart.

In Europe you had to go to elementary school at age seven. Coming from *Cheder*, I didn't know what to do in school, and so my parents hired private tutors for me. Every year, as I got older, I had a different teacher. My teachers were all women, and they would come over to our house for my lessons. I had to learn how to read in Yiddish, Hebrew and Polish. Later on I picked up Russian, Ukrainian and Czech, and of course, many years later – English. I had a good head for languages, and for learning. My father and mother were very impressed. They wanted me to learn and to be smart. When I came home from school with the report card, I got a lot of hugs and kisses and smiles. I had a very happy childhood.

Holidays in Ozierany

Many of my most cherished memories are of the holidays in my hometown. These were truly special days, when everyone and everything around me took on an aura of reverence and festivity. On Lag ba'Omer, the Jewish teachers would take all their Jewish students out on a picnic. We didn't have a bonfire for fear of starting a forest fire in the heavily wooded areas, but we picked flowers and sang. It was a wonderful time. Rosh Hashanah was another beautiful holiday, marked by a feast prepared by my mother. On Hanukkah we had sweets and nuts.

I was very picky about what I ate. On Purim, the only *hamantashen* I would eat were the prune-filled ones. If they had anything but prunes inside, I wouldn't eat them. If I didn't like something, I wouldn't touch it. On Passover, I remember feeling hungry. My mother would say to me, "Rochale, what do you want to eat?" She would then list all kinds of foods that we were allowed to eat, but I didn't like any of them. She would get exasperated and ask me, "So what do you want, my child?" And the way she said it, I knew she was angry at me. Yet she would never yell or make me feel bad.

There was one treat in particular that she kept offering to me, but I always refused. Years later, long after I lost her, I was shopping in a drugstore in America and I saw this same treat on the shelf. I felt that I had to try it; my mother had offered it to me my whole life and I had never given it a chance. I bought the treat, but I never got through the first bite.

Dreams fly away

As a child, I was fascinated with sewing. I wanted to learn how to do it, but my mother wouldn't let me. She had a cousin who was a seamstress. When this cousin's husband died, she was forced to work as a seamstress to support her eleven children. My mother didn't want that for me. She didn't want me to have a trade; she wanted me to marry a man who could provide for me. That's the way it was back then.

I shed tears over her insistence and cried that I wanted to be a seamstress. My dream was to go beyond the role of a simple seamstress and to become a decorator, putting colors together. But I could only dream about that, and even those dreams flew away when the Germans came. Until this very day, I don't know how to sew a button.

SAM, IN THE GHETTO

Ribbentrop-Molotov

The fate of my hometown of Turzysk, as well as all of Volhynia, was sealed on August 23, 1939. On this date, Nazi Germany and the Soviet Union signed a non-aggression pact, named after the two countries' respective foreign ministers at the time, Joachim Von Ribbentrop and Vyacheslav Molotov. By the secret terms of the pact, it was agreed that Poland would be partitioned into three major areas: the Warthland area bordering Germany would be annexed outright to the German Reich, and all non-German inhabitants expelled to the east; the central area would become a German protectorate governed by a German civil authority; and over 77,000 square miles of eastern Polish lands, with a population of twelve million (including Turzysk), would become Russian territory.

At the young age of fourteen, I was completely unaware of the major events that would redefine my existence. I knew nothing of what was going on in the world around me. I had yet to hear the name Hitler. We didn't read the newspapers in 1939, but even if we had kept up with current events, we could not have foreseen the unfolding of history or the sudden outbreak of the war that swallowed our town whole.

On September 1, 1939, Hitler's forces invaded Poland from

the west. According to plan, Soviet troops invaded Polish territory from the east on September 17, 1939. Poland surrendered a mere ten days later, on September 27. The next day, Poland was partitioned in accordance with the treaty, ending a brief twenty-year period as an independent nation. The whole of Volhynia, including Turzysk, was annexed by the Soviet Union.

We were caught in the inevitable tide of political scheming, imperialistic aspirations, strategic alliances and subsequent betrayals of the Second World War. Our lives changed in an instant, and it would not be the last time such an earthquake shook Turzysk.

Working for the Russians

We went from Polish to Russian rule seemingly overnight, yet if that had been the extent of our wartime turbulence, we would have been well off. I myself had nothing to fear from the Communists, since we were not avid capitalists. I didn't speak Russian, but I spoke Ukrainian, and so I was able to understand some of their language. I was young, and able to adapt easily to shifting circumstances. I had done it before with my father's death, and I could do it again with our new rulers.

The Russians were quick to implement their Communist doctrine, and immediately took from the rich. In addition, they pursued a policy of liquidation of the Jewish parties, organizations and institutions. One of the Turzysk youth movements went underground, and its members arranged to escape to Vilna, in Lithuania. The Russians were so thorough in disassembling our way of life that they even removed all the *taleisim* [Jewish prayer shawls] from the synagogues, simply because they didn't know what they were.

Everybody in town was affected. We all lost our businesses. For my immediate family, this wasn't much of a change. My grandmother lost ownership of her bakery, but she continued to work there, baking for the Russians. My grandfather continued to sew, but now he was sewing for the Russian soldiers, mending their uniforms and clothes. My sisters and I were put to work for the Russians as well. They appointed us jobs on the railroad that stretched from Poland to Russia. It was heavy, physical work, carrying supplies on our shoulders, but my sisters braved it alongside me. We were not paid much, but it was enough to provide for our mother. We had food, and for that we were thankful.

However, there were restrictions on our movement. We didn't dare go visit my father's grave in Masiv, and I lost all contact with my father's sisters; to this day I do not know what became of them. We were afraid, and we were being watched. Going to the villages was forbidden, yet it was a risk we had to take in order to maintain our lives, and so we kept our excursions to the necessary bare minimum.

We used to go out to the country and bring back bags of corn from the farmers to make flour. Though they were our occupiers, the Russians also supplied us with a cow and sheep. Compared to how the Germans were to behave in the same capacity, the Russians were very good to us. Though I was quite young, I understood the importance of nurturing my connections with them. They liked vodka and whiskey, and I was more than happy to produce some for them. In this way, a relationship was formed between us, and when I needed something from them, they would give it to me.

I had already learned the ways of barter and marketing, importing and exporting, and I knew how to buy a little here and sell a little there. My salesman efforts brought me in contact with many non-Jewish people. The Gentiles knew we were Jewish, and on their part they were openly antisemitic. But at the time, we had Stalin on our side. By his orders, we were called "Yevrei" and not "Jews." He implemented a level of respect towards us. They were afraid to touch us.

"Yevrei, run away!"

During the two years of Russian occupation, 1939 through 1941, many Jewish refugees managed to make their way from the volatile German zone of Poland to the safer Russian zone. The partitioning of Poland had brought the Nazi killing machine upon them years before it devoured us as well, and these refugees were hungry and frightened. The people of Turzysk took them into the synagogue and fed them, and it was not too long before my town became a sort of center for these Jews.

The refugees came with firsthand accounts of the horrors. We learned from them that the Germans had taken over, and abused and tortured Jews. We were no longer blind to the reality. The Russians urged the refugees to become Russian citizens. Those that refused were sent to Siberia.

The refugees' stories had their effect. A lot of people chose to flee further into Russia. Around this time I witnessed a sight I'll never forget. A Russian captain, who was Jewish, stood in the middle of our city and screamed at the top of his lungs for all to hear, "Yevrei, run away from here! I'll give you buses! Go! The Germans are coming!" The Russians had been there and witnessed the Germans in action. This captain was willing to supply transportation, a true testament to his desperation.

My sisters and I were already packed, our belongings all collected into a little box and ready to go. It was our grandparents who stopped us. My grandfather said, "Who are you going to run to, the Bolsheviks? In the First World War, the Germans came and they didn't do anything to us. They were good to us."

Their experiences from the previous war, which had ended a little over twenty years before, convinced them that nothing would happen to them. The younger people, who found the refugee accounts more compelling than the older generation's fond memories of the Germans, were eager to run. But at that time you listened to your father, and so my mother listened to hers. When the Jewish captain's buses left Turzysk, my family and I were not on them.

The Germans crash the party

The Ribbentrop-Molotov Pact served Hitler's interests for nearly two years, after which he did not hesitate to betray his so-called allies and launch an attack. Nazi Germany's invasion of the Soviet Union began in the dead of a midsummer's night, at 3:15 a.m. on June 22, 1941. Stalin had ignored several warnings that Germany was likely to attack, and had ordered no full-scale mobilization of forces. As a result, the territories gained by the Soviet Union with the Ribbentrop-Molotov Pact were lost in a matter of weeks. Within six months, the Soviet military had suffered losses of about 4.5 million casualties and prisoners combined.

Turzysk fell into German hands within six days of their invasion into Russia. On Saturday, June 28, 1941, the Jewish youth held a dance for young men and women, as they did every Saturday night. The dances were festive, joyful events with food and drinks, but that night would be different. At midnight the Germans marched into Turzysk. They appeared in full uniform, and one could say they wore their intentions on their sleeves. Bombs fell on the city, and gunfire was frantically exchanged between the Russian and the German soldiers. Russian soldiers ran in the streets. One soldier raced off in his underwear. The German soldier who had walked Reisel home recognized her and tore her away from us. She returned later, badly shaken.

The terror intensified over the next few days. The Ukrainians were horribly eager to cooperate with the Germans. Several of them accompanied the Nazi soldiers and showed them who was a Jew and who wasn't. They were more than happy to point out where Jews lived, and were heard joyously shouting antisemitic slurs and threats.

My family stayed put. We couldn't move, let alone leave the city. We hid under our beds. The streets were unsafe; going out was out of the question. The Ukrainians were all over the place, and they were on the lookout. There was nothing we could do but wait.

Dawn of the ghetto

The Germans won control of Turzysk without much of a fight. Their first order of business was to establish a ghetto that would confine the movement of the city's Jewish population. An area was set within the town, which engulfed the synagogues and the Yiddish schools. Our house was already within this radius, and so we awoke to find our beloved neighborhood had become an open-air prison. We were living in the ghetto and we were to die in the ghetto. We understood we would be there until they killed us.

Confining us Jews to the ghetto was not enough for the Germans. Every Jew was required to wear a yellow "Star of David" sewn onto the front, the sleeve and the back of one's clothes. Jewish homes were required to have the yellow star painted on their walls. We were all forced to mark ourselves in this humiliating manner, and in order to ensure a begrudging cooperation, the Germans immediately established a local Ukrainian police force under their direction. Not long after, the Germans required the assembly of a Judenrat (Jewish council) for Turzysk as well. Our situation was horrible, and we were thankful for only one thing: we weren't being killed – at least not yet.

Slaves of the German war machine

All able-bodied Jews, men and women alike, were to report daily to the railroad yards. German trains and Russian trains had different wheel bases, which meant that the German trains had to have their wheels changed in order to supply the German army with equipment as they deepened their invasion into Russia. The task of changing these wheels was forced upon us, the Jews of Turzysk. Some of the men were taken to the forest to cut down trees, and others brought the trees back to the railroad station. Ultimately the trees were loaded onto trains returning to Germany. All forced labor in Turzysk was geared toward supporting the German war effort, a fact that made it that much more terrible for all of us. We were forced to be part of the very machine that was destroying us.

I had already been working the railroad tracks under Russian rule. My mother made me look older for this purpose by having me wear long pants, a long jacket and a hat. She wanted me to look twenty years old instead of sixteen. I continued at the railroad for another year under the Germans, until 1942. Work conditions were harsher under the Nazis. They were brutal supervisors, who dispensed violence at will. During that time, I picked up some German from hearing it spoken.

My sisters were seamstresses by then, sewing uniforms and suits for the German soldiers, as well as clothes for their wives. The arrival of the Germans marked the end for my grandparents. Grandmother's bakery was gone, and so was grandfather's tailor shop. They sat around, waiting for death.

Hunger and fear

Food had become so scarce that the children and teenagers would often sneak out of the ghetto at night in search of any morsel they could get their hands on. Leaving the ghetto, however, was punishable by death. Each time I escaped our prison, I knew I was putting myself in danger, but it was a necessary risk. I would rip the Star of David off my jacket and make a run for the countryside. I knew some Gentile families there who were kind enough to give me food, which I then brought back to my family. My heart beat as if would jump out of my chest every time I did this. I did not know at that time that I would be running for my life for years to come.

Hunger and fear were constantly battling within me. When the hunger overpowered the fear, I would go in the middle of the day. The Germans shot at me as I ran out of the ghetto. Though I was lucky enough to avoid getting shot, I could not always avoid the Germans altogether. When I was caught under the suspicion that I had intended to leave the ghetto, the Germans took off my pants and whipped me. The pain and humiliation have stayed with me to this day.

We were treated like dogs by the local Ukrainians as well, who enjoyed their new standing under Germany's racist hierarchy and felt free to rob the Turzysk Jews of their possessions. We were not being exterminated – not yet – but death had become a part of our lives.

For a while, the Ukrainians and the Polish militia posed a more imminent threat than the Germans themselves. Their antisemitism was free to run wild, and not a day went by without a Jew being killed. Girls were in constant danger of rape. My mother was terribly worried about my older sisters Chasia and Reisel, who were eighteen and nineteen years old at the time and very beautiful. In order to protect them, my mother would cover their faces with the soot and tar from the fireplace so they would look dirty and ugly. She prayed that this would allow them to be left untouched.

The Germans loaded up trucks with young Jewish girls, and they never came back. Some of the girls jumped out of second floor windows and killed themselves when they saw the Germans coming. My oldest sister Chasia was married, and for the time being they allowed her, as well as my other sisters, to stay with us, but we still had much to fear.

German soldiers would enter our ghetto on weekends in search of a thrill. The Ukrainians would point out the Jewish homes to them, and the Germans would then go door to door, seek out girls that were to their liking and rape them. My dear mother was at least able to spare my sisters this horror. As soon as the Germans saw my sisters covered up in soot and dirt, they would kick them, urinate on them and spit on them, but they did not rape them. I stood and watched my sisters go through this violent humiliation, and I was powerless to put a stop to it. Worse than the hunger or the constant fear of death was the fire that burned within me over being unable to help my family.

The brick factory

On the outskirts of Turzysk stood a brick factory that had been owned by the Walner family for 130 years. The bricks were air-dried, and a key part of the manufacturing process was the excavation of clay. The factory had been operational for generations, and by that fateful summer of 1942 the excavated area was deep and very wide. What my family and I did not know was that on August 20, 1942, a ransom demand was made, but the Jews of Turzysk could not meet the German demands. It is doubtful if it would have made a difference.

Three days later, on August 23, 1942, we were gathered in the center of town: myself along with my grandmother Bassia, my grandfather Mort Hirsch Opeliner, my mother Rochel Bojmel, my sisters Reisel and Malka, my married sister Chasia, my brother-in-law Motel Perkel and their two-month-old son, Zelig Perkel, my uncles Schlomo, Yonah and Leibel Opeliner, their families, and the other Jewish residents of Turzysk. We stood with suitcases in our hands and hope in our hearts. The Germans had promised us that we would be relocated to the city of Kowel for work, with the excuse there was no more work in Turzysk. A palpable thrill rippled through the crowd. We had been suffering for so long that the prospect of a new life was intoxicating.

We began the arduous, grueling walk towards Kowel along the cobblestone streets. Ukrainian police escorts watched over us, as well as German soldiers. As we reached the outskirts of Turzysk, we were suddenly turned uphill toward the Walner brick factory. Something was not right. Why were we walking towards the brick factory instead of Kowel? The situation was now marked by fear, as realization swept through us: we were being herded toward our own deaths. Panic surged. Shrieking and wailing grew louder and louder. I can still hear the shrill screams in my head. They have never left me.

What I saw

Ours was a march toward death, and many were killed on the way. I saw rabbis being taken by the Gestapo, their beards cut off and their bodies beaten to a bloody pulp. I saw pregnant women shot right in front of me. The girls had all been ordered to strip naked. I saw my sister Chasia holding on to her baby boy and a slim prayer. She frantically covered the baby with a piece of paper because they were taking the babies away. The Ukrainians rode up on their horses, grabbed the babies as if they were nothing more than tattered old

dolls, and threw them in a wagon. I saw many of the babies slip
through the cracks in the bed of the wagon and fall underneath,
where they were trampled to death by the horses. The Ukrainians
had us younger boys crawl behind the horses to pick up the bodies of
the dead babies and throw them in the grave. That was to be the last
job we would do for the Germans.

Chasia was able to hold on to her baby boy for just a little
bit longer, before he was noticed by a soldier and snatched from
her arms. She looked on as he was thrown into the wagon with the
others. We had reached our grave by then, and were standing beside
it. Chasia recognized her baby boy just above the horse's leg, and ran
toward him. My mother screamed: "Chasi, why are you running?" I
saw the tears that streaked down her face. I was crying too. Chasia
caught up with the wagon. She grabbed her baby, still alive, clutched
him to her breast and covered him up with the paper again.

I saw my sister run back to the graves, back to us. And so
did the Ukrainians. I saw them grab her by the grave. I watched as
they took away the piece of paper that she had hoped would hide
her baby. Chasia screamed at them in Ukrainian and in Polish and in
German, "Please don't kill my baby! Kill me!" Then I saw them beat
her with sticks. Her words meant nothing to them. All they said was,
"You'll be dead too." I saw them tear her baby away from her breast
and throw him in the grave. I saw my baby nephew die. They said,
"Now we're going to throw you in on top of the baby." I saw them
grab her by the breast, throw her on top of the baby and shoot her. I
saw my sister die.

A mother's love

I remember that day clearly. I will never forget it. And I will never
understand it. Some of these murderers had once been our neighbors.
How could they do this to us?

Surrounded by madness and slaughter, my mother turned to
me. She grabbed me by the arm and said, "Shulem, my child, take
my sweater. I don't want you to catch a cold." I took the sweater from

her. She said, "In a minute you'll be in the grave next to me. Run, my child! Run!" I was paralyzed with fear. I didn't know where to go. My mother told me to go to Rastov, to Petro. He was a Gentile who had always been good to us. She tore off my yellow Star of David. "If you live through the war, don't forget where you came from!"

I obeyed her, and I ran. I ran as fast as I could. Shots were fired at me, but I did not stop. My mother and Reisel were pushed into a grave. They weren't shot at; they were still alive and dirt was being thrown on top of them. Malka tried to run with me, but a bullet caught her, killing her in an instant. I know if I had just grabbed for her, I could have gotten her into a safe place. But I did not stop.

This was a defining moment of my life. I became a different person, no longer a teenage boy. I had no other choice but to fight for my life and to survive. Suddenly, I was an adult, and I had only one option left: to move as fast as possible. I ran into the fields and hid among the corn stalks. I felt sick, but I couldn't let that slow me down. I was alone and afraid, cold and hungry, and I had only myself to rely on. Night fell, and the darkness revealed one last horrible sight. In the distance I saw our ghetto in flames.

On that day, the Jews from Turzysk and other Jews from the surrounding towns, shtetls, and villages were all murdered, their bodies thrown into the massive grave site at the Walner brick factory. My mother, my grandparents, my sisters, my nephew, my brother-in-law, my uncles and their families were among the victims.

RACHEL, IN THE GHETTO

This is Russia now

I was fourteen years old when the Russians arrived, and to my young eyes it seemed that life as we knew it had come to a sudden, violent halt. We had not been killed, but our lives were over. People went into hiding, and all were afraid to let the Russians know what their professions had once been in what was now regarded as their previous incarnation. Many people were sent to Siberia, a horrific threat that hung over everybody's head like a guillotine.

I no longer went to school. Instead I sat around the house and read books all day long. My older brother Meyer, aged seventeen, was young and ready to work, but there was nothing for him to do. His restless, eager nature was forced into an unnatural state of stillness.

My father's business was over. No longer free to come and go to Warsaw, he had no way of procuring his merchandise. He was forced to adapt quickly to a new reality if he was to keep providing for us. I cannot remember what he did after that, but I imagine it was undertaken in an air of desperation. While we were all mostly confined to our home for lack of any other options, Father would often be gone, out getting food any way he could while avoiding the Russians.

Food had gone from plenty to scarce. The day after the Russians arrived we had absolutely nothing to eat. We couldn't buy white bread or flour. The stores were cleaned out, the shelves lay empty. We turned to the Czech people who lived in the small villages nearby. They understood the situation all too well, and were kind enough to allow us access to their fruit trees. We picked cherries, apples and all that we could get our hands on. In this way, we had everything we needed during those first, hard days of transition.

I strongly disliked the Russians. They would use our *talleisim* as shawls or nightgowns against the cold. It hurt me to see our religious articles defamed like that. They supplied us with cornflour, which we were to use for baking our own bread, but for the life of me, I couldn't stomach a single bite of it. No matter how long you baked the cornflour bread, when you took it out of the oven you could still squeeze water out of it. My brothers purchased white flour from non-Jews, but given the circumstances it was of low quality too.

Throughout all of this we never thought of running away. We did not know that the Germans were coming. We thought that we were living in Russia now, and the hardships this new citizenship entailed were a simple fact of life.

The Promised Land

One question was on our minds and lips at the time: "Why don't we have a Jewish country?" Though I was young, I became quite preoccupied with this notion. I had heard the name Palestine. Starting with my early studies in the *Cheder* and continuing through my plentiful reading, I had always been very interested in our religion. God's liberation of the Jews from Egypt was my favorite biblical story, and it fascinated me then more than ever.

Being the smart rabbi that he was, my grandfather was asked these questions many times, well before the Russian occupation. His answer, invariably, was, "Yes, there is going to be a Yiddisheh land," but only after Jewish blood will run like the ocean." He was well read in the Torah, and his statement that the Jewish Land would follow a holocaust was a grim prediction that his many students took to heart.

My grandfather did not live to see his prophecy fulfilled. Years later, I visited Israel for the first time. Upon my arrival in Tel Aviv, shortly after the War of Independence, word spread from one person to the other that a grandchild of Yossele Zanches, as he was known to his students, was in Israel. The students sat with me and told me stories about my grandfather and my mother. Many of them had left for Palestine before the war, as early as 1933, as *halutzim* (pioneers). Israel was the land that God had promised to the Jewish People, but also the land that my grandfather had promised to me and to his students.

Kept in the dark

The Russian occupation lasted for two years. During these times we were kept in the dark, especially us children. My parents wanted to spare us the news of horrors taking place elsewhere. They held on to hope until the very last minute.

My town took in refugees from the areas in Poland that had been taken over by the Germans in accordance with the Ribbentrop-Molotov Pact. These refugees never had it as good anywhere else; we treated them like brothers. We took them in with open arms and gave them whatever we could. I believe they shared their stories about the Germans and what they had seen, but not with the children. I had only the vaguest of ideas, and nothing was certain in my mind, not until the Germans arrived. This innocence was lost forever in June of 1941.

Out of the clear blue sky

I do not know whether others around me, my family included, had any indication of what was to come. I experienced it all as if it came out of the clear blue sky, much like the bombs that landed on Kiev. This news came to us over the radio: Kiev had been bombed on June 22, 1941, as the war between Germany and the Soviet Union erupted. We were about to be engulfed by the fighting. We packed up and headed for Russia.

Our only mode of transportation was our feet. We were going to walk as far as we could into Russia, far away from the Germans. My uncle Mendel had an advantage – he loaded his whole family onto his buggy, and they drove away. They succeeded in fleeing deep into Russia, but we were not as lucky. After traveling by foot for a couple of days, it was clear that we were caught in between the two fighting armies with nowhere to go. Seeing we had no choice, we turned back.

In our absence, the Germans had picked out the twelve best young men of our town, the highest hopes of our next generation, and executed them. Their bodies lay in the water along our route, a silent warning to all who entered and all who left. My parents cried. I cried too, but without tears. I was already changing, adapting to my new existence. My heart was hardening.

Nowhere to run

My body ached with the urge to run. There was nothing I wanted more than to flee, to be elsewhere, but there was nowhere we could go. How could we run? Where could we run to? There were no opportunities. Our nights were sleepless. I sat up tight and vigilant, like a watchdog. Our neighbors sat with us. We sought each other's company. I was a sixteen-year-old girl, and I was sure the Germans would come and take me away. The prospect horrified me.

It was only matter of a few days before Germans filled the town. They didn't make a ghetto right away. Their first action was to force all the townspeople, men and women, girls and boys alike, to work for them. We cleaned closets at the train stations and shoveled snow. I was taken to clean snow as well. My brother

Meyer had been assigned the job before me, and he was there to watch out for me. He had met a German who was very nice, and he approached him and pleaded, "I've got one sister. She's too young to work." This German soldier filled out papers for me so that I didn't have to go to work.

After about three weeks, we were caged in the ghetto. Our town's synagogue remained outside the borders of the newly established ghetto. The Jews barely managed to save the holy Torah books before the Ukrainian people came in and took the whole synagogue apart. It was gone so quickly, it seemed to have disappeared. We understood that what they had done to our house of prayer was what they wished to do to us – erase our existence.

Along with the enforcement of the ghetto was the requirement that we wear a Jewish yellow star, but I never wore one. I didn't want to, and I was not afraid to refuse. In its first days, when the ghetto was not yet closed, I used to run out to the farmers for whatever my mother wanted. I would put on clothes like our non-Jewish neighbors, peasant clothes, but I still looked Jewish. I could not hide my heritage. The farmers not only knew I was Jewish, but also that I had nothing to give them in return, yet I was never forced to beg. They understood without words the reason I had risked my life to come to them, and they gave me food as soon as I showed up.

A girl in the ghetto

As a young girl in the ghetto, I was deathly afraid of the Germans. Whenever I saw a German approach, I felt as though I might die on the spot. My stomach would clench, and my heart would beat so hard it made me dizzy. My mother put me in rags, cut my hair and made my face dirty, so that when a German saw me he wouldn't want to rape me, but this only accentuated my fear. The threat of rape was very real.

Bomber planes came down upon our city. Ozierany had no

tall buildings, and when the bombers came, they flew so low it felt like they were right on top of us. When they flew so close, they had no need for their bombs; they could simply mow people down with bullets. We ran away from them and headed for the dense trees, so that they wouldn't see us. Once we were hiding in a cluster of tree trunks when we were surprised by a tall German soldier. He was hiding from the planes, just as we were. He walked toward us.

My mother noticed that this soldier was eating me up with his eyes. She knew immediately what was on this man's mind, and once the planes had cleared the sky she didn't hesitate. She said to me, "Rochaleh, run away."

I ran, and the German soldier bolted after me. He was on my heels. I ran by three houses, and when I got to the fourth house I ducked inside. Luckily, he didn't see me enter. It was a family of non-Jews, with children who were the same age as me. When I appeared in their home, I hid the fact that I had been running for my life and that there had been a German soldier on my tail. I pretended I'd come by for a play date, the way I used to when we were younger. They suspected nothing.

Under the bed, behind locked doors

Following that close call, I went into hiding. I spent a week burrowed underneath a Jewish neighbor's bed, my muscles cramped and my mind racing. After a week, I took a risk and moved to Mizocz, a neighboring village. My family was well-acquainted with a man there by the name of Shulem, who owned a local barber shop. Shulem's family had known me since I was born, and they did not want to see me get hurt.

I was locked in a dark little hiding place in the back of his store, where I could at least stretch my body and stand up. There were no doors or windows. My mother was aware of my whereabouts, and she arranged for food to be brought to me. Other than that, I was alone. I remained there, in the dark, for three weeks.

The ghetto's end

While the Jews of my town rejoiced with the Torah on the eve of the holiday of Simchat Torah, I was overcome with confusion and anger. I could not understand how they still rejoiced. I cannot decide whether I was rebelling against religion or against the passivity that I recognized around me. I did not know exactly what it was, only that I did not understand my Jewish brothers and sisters. I didn't like the fact that nobody had anything to fight with. We all stayed in the ghetto and did nothing about it. Everybody had something to eat, but our lives were miserable.

The Germans had chosen Simchat Torah to end our ghetto. They waited until it was dark. I watched as one of the German soldiers came in to the synagogue and beat one of the Jewish Judenrat officials. I saw blood in his eyes.

The Germans started busting their way into houses, one by one. My parents yelled to us, "Go out, go out!" I ran out to the backyard. The ghetto was closed off by then with three kinds of barbed wire. I don't know how I crawled through them all, but I did it, and I ran out of the ghetto. As I did so, I was filled with rage: we could have cut those wires to prepare ourselves for this event, but nobody did.

The wires cut my skin, and I was bleeding. My parents had seen me run off; they knew I was trying to escape. As I ran, my mother ran with my brothers. She was crying because as she ran, she came across other people who had seen me. Whoever recognized me could see that I was bleeding, and knowing that there was gunfire all around me, they were sure that I had been shot. Nobody wanted to be the one to tell my mother that her daughter had been killed, but she began to piece this together from people's fractured accounts.

While other people saw me, I saw no one. I was running, and I knew nothing else but that. I said to myself, and to God, "If you don't want me to live, let them kill me from behind, not from the front, so I don't have to see them." I had this thought many times in the next chapter of my life. I would not stand still and be killed;

they would not get that satisfaction from me. I would not look into the eyes of my murderers. I would die running.

Countless Jews died that night. My father was among them, but we didn't know it at the time. Even afterward, we didn't know where it had happened or how. We couldn't go back to the ghetto. Our father was gone. All was lost.

SAM, RUNNING AND HIDING

Petro

The night my family was murdered, I slept on the hard ground somewhere between Turzysk and Rastov. My mother's sweater kept me from freezing. Without it I surely would have fallen ill, though I could not truly feel the cold, not on that night. I felt nothing. Everything had been taken from me in a brutal instant, and all that was left was shock and fear. I could not mourn my family or my own loss of innocence. All I could do was run and hide. I waited until nightfall the next day and got back on my feet.

Were it not for Petro, I would have had nowhere to run, no sanctuary in mind to keep my legs going. Petro, short for Petrivna Tokarsky, was a non-Jewish landowner from Rastov who had longstanding ties with my family. Back in better times, when my grandmother Bassia still had her bakery and ran her fresh produce market, Petro was one of the farmers from whom she had bought fruit. My uncle Leibel had also worked for Petro many times, performing carpentry jobs for him. It was on these trips with my uncle Leibel that I came to know him as well. When the Turzysk ghetto had closed in on us, Petro was one of the farmers I would run to at night, and he would always give me bread and potatoes.

It was late at night when I finally arrived at his house. I had been afraid to approach any earlier, and I was still afraid. Petro had a wife and a daughter, Nina, and there was no assurance that they would be as forthcoming as he was. Yet I had no choice. I snuck up to his window, making sure that nobody saw me. I knocked, and Petro ran out to me.

We were both crying. Petro was amazed that I had made it out alive. He'd been to Turzysk, and he had seen the carnage with his own eyes. He believed everyone was dead. He said, "Child, what are you going to do now? How are you going to live now? They're going to kill you!"

I cried, "Petro, help me! Please!"

With tears in his eyes, he humbly replied, "I'll do my best."

His best was more than I could have hoped for in such bleak times. Petro was a good man, and my mother had recognized this quality within him. She trusted Petro so much that in a moment of great peril, with only seconds to spare, his name was one of the last things she said to me. And although Petro had made no promise to my mother, his actions were always those of total dedication. I owe my life to his bravery, his kindness, his personal risk and sacrifice. As I've often felt my mother looking down upon me, I know that she looked down upon Petro as well.

I had an uncle

Petro brought me in to his house, sat me next to the warm stove and fed me hot food. Once I was feeling better, it was time to move me into hiding. We both understood that having me in his house was too dangerous for him, his family and myself. Petro dug a hiding hole for me out in his barn amongst the horses and the cows. It would not be as warm and cozy as his home, but it would be safe.

The next evening, Petro and I were both shocked by the arrival of an unexpected guest: Leibel Opeliner, my uncle. I was overcome with joy to have at least one of my family members at my side. Leibel brought grim news: he had seen our entire family killed, his own wife and children included. He had survived and done as I had, and had come to Petro and offered his services in exchange for food and shelter. With my help, we would both install new windows in Petro's house. I was grateful for the opportunity to repay Petro's kindness in any meager way that I could.

And so I had an uncle. To keep the both of us hidden, Petro helped us dig a hole four feet deep under the pig pen. This was to be our new home. During the day we installed windows and at night we slept and ate in our hole in the ground. Petro's house was far enough from the road and distant enough from its nearest neighbors that Leibel and I could pass as ordinary workers.

This was our life for the next three months. Between work and hiding, Uncle Leibel and I made additional little holes for use as lookouts. We had to be vigilant and keep watch for soldiers. They were known for hunting runaway Jews and the people who were hiding them. At no time did we believe ourselves to be safe. Every day without incident was a blessing. At any given moment, even this relative freedom of sleeping under the pigs could be taken away from us.

Leibel understood this. On more than one occasion, he said to me, "We can't stay here." His mind was constantly searching for a plan. Finally, an opportunity arose. Leibel came in contact with three other Jewish survivors from Turzysk who were hiding in Rastov. He said, "If we got together, the five of us, we could go to Ludmir (Wlodzimierz Wolynski). It's still a Jewish ghetto, and I've heard they haven't killed people there."

The five of us departed for Ludmir in the dead of night. We were spotted by a few Ukrainians who had approached the road from the other direction. They stopped us and asked, "Jews, where are you going?" When they heard of our destination, they warned us against our plan. "Yesterday they killed everybody there," they said. Leibel and I had no choice but to return to Petro's sanctuary, but the three young Jewish men had reached their breaking points. They said they couldn't live that kind of life and had decided to head back to Turzysk. "Maybe if we go back, they won't kill us," the men said with faint hope in their voices. They followed through on their suicidal plan and were killed immediately upon entering their old hometown.

Once again there were just the two of us; my uncle Leibel and me.

My uncle's childhood friends

Petro was horrified by the cruel fate that befell their Jewish neighbors who had been fortunate enough to survive the Turzysk executions. That they were still hunted down like animals was against everything Petro believed in. In an effort to make a change for the better, he slaughtered a pig and sent it to the local Rastov magistrate. Afterwards, he met with him to suggest that they establish an organization to hide their surviving Jewish neighbors. The magistrate politely declined. He said, "We know how to deal with the Jewish problem – now go and mind your own business." They next day the slaughtered pig was sent back to Petro.

Perhaps it was then that the Ukrainian policemen began to suspect that Petro might be doing more than suggesting, and was actively participating in sheltering runaway Jews. The Germans had promised the Polish and Ukrainian policemen a reward of five pounds of sugar for every Jew captured. Back then, this was considered a fortune, and only strengthened their motivation to hunt us down.

They came in the middle of a cold November day in 1942. Ukrainian policemen surrounded Petro's home and began to chant, "Jews come out! Jews come out!" When I imagine their coarse voices shouting in unison, a chill still runs down my spine. The barn was constructed of wood with a straw roof, and Uncle Leibel was able to peer below through the slats in the loft. From his vantage point he recognized faces from his childhood. He had known some of the Ukrainian policemen since they had all been little boys; he had played with some and worked for others.

Leibel said to me, "Shulem, I'm going out to them. I know them. We were raised together." He felt confident that once they saw him, they would feel differently, and he could then convince them not to harm us. I don't know how, but in the pit of my stomach I knew better.

I begged him to stay, saying, "Uncle, don't go. I'm not going, I'm staying."

He said, "If you stay they'll kill you. We can't stay; they're going to burn down the barn."

I could not stop my uncle; he was older than me and his mind was set. He left the barn intent on dealing with them. I saw him crawl out and prayed for his safety. The next few moments felt like hours. Then I heard the gun shots. They had murdered him without hesitation. I peeked through the side of the barn and there was my uncle's body on the ground, covered in blood.

The Ukrainian policemen, who had known my uncle Leibel since they were little boys, were busy burying his body near the side of the house. They placed a wooden crucifix and a Star of David in front of Petro's barn and set it on fire, thinking I was still inside. I jumped onto the roof of the barn and ran into the Rastov forest once again. To this day, it is hard for me to believe that I was able to escape them.

Up in the tree

I ran into the bushes that lined the garden. My body was scraped and cut, my skin stinging. From there I crawled into the woods unseen, but I knew I could not stop there. I chose a tree that I believed could support my weight and climbed up its branches, as high as I could possibly go. I remained in that tree for a few days, while they kept looking for me. They had realized that I'd escaped, and they wouldn't let up. I could see them all from the treetop. I saw young Ukrainian and Polish children gleefully join in the search. It was a game to them. It seemed to me as if the entire village of Rastov had volunteered to take part in my manhunt. All they had to do was look up, and they would see me. There were many times when I was sure it had to happen, and I was breathless with relief when it didn't.

Petro and his daughter Nina were forced to run as well. Their ways parted in the process. Nina stayed with relatives on their farm for two weeks before returning home. Upon her return she was arrested by the Ukrainian militia. She was taken in front of a tribunal, stripped naked and sentenced to execution for giving refuge to Jews. She pleaded for her life. Moments before the execution, the Ukrainian militia abruptly left. It was neither the first nor the last time that tragedy and miracle occurred side by side, equally defying our understanding.

Living in barns

I was running out of ways to survive. Even though my presence had already cost him his barn and put him at great risk, I returned to Petro. I was young, afraid and all alone; I had nowhere else to turn. He never complained about the danger I had brought upon him. He mourned Leibel's death as I had.

When I showed up, he said, "You should go to another village. I know some Czechs in a nearby village. They are good to Jews." I was barefoot and half-naked, and I didn't want to wander out in search of kind people amongst the monsters. Petro said, "Don't worry, I'll take you there myself when it's nighttime." He walked me over to the neighboring village and pointed out the house. He said, "These are good people."

I knocked on the door, hoping for the best. One look at me was enough for them to understand who I was. "You're Jewish," they said.

"Yes. Can I stay here, with your cows?"

They answered me with a shrug. "Well, you can stay, but if they catch you, there's nothing we can do. They're looking for Jews, you know."

And so I was taken in. The family hid me in their barn for a few weeks and supplied me with food and water.

When they calculated that the risk was getting too high, they sent me off to another Czech family. Perhaps they were relatives or close friends. This second Czech man was very nervous. "I can't keep you anymore," he said to me. "People will start to talk here." Both Czech families were now too afraid to take a risk for a young teenage boy they did not know.

I moved only by night, and once again put my faith in Petro. He had never turned me down. This time he took a bigger risk and brought me into the house. I crawled up in the warmth and lay there all night. I was worn out, running and hiding and fearing for my life every waking moment.

Petro had a new idea for me. He said, "You know, I know a woman not too far from here. She lives with her sister. Her sister is a bit crazy, but they are nice people. They will take you in." The sisters were Ukrainian. It was never said outright, but I believe that Petro was in a romantic relationship with one of the two sisters. Only she knew about me. They were farmers, and they owned about fifty cows. Petro asked her, "Please, let him work for you with the cows when your sister leaves the house."

The sister that Petro had referred to as the crazy one was roughly my size, and so I was given her clothes to disguise myself. I looked like a female Ukrainian farmer; I wore a skirt and I covered my face with a scarf. I was too young at the time to even grow a beard. I slept with the cows, and I used to go out with them every morning at 5 a.m. The sister would visit me in the afternoon with a little bit of food. She was very kind to me, and warned me not to take the cows close to the roads because the Ukrainians walked there.

This arrangement lasted for about two months. I knew it was bound to end. One morning, as I walked the cows, I was spotted. I looked up and saw the Ukrainian ruffians walking towards me. The words, "This is the end," went through my mind as I ran. They ran after me immediately as I entered the woods, but they were not deterred. Some farmers with lands near the woods had gardens, and they grew high bushes and put wires on top of them to keep thieves and vandals away. I jumped through the wires without hesitation. The cuts and bleeding were a small price to pay for my life. The Ukrainian policemen didn't even think of looking there. I had lost them.

The hole in the ground

Petro told me what I had already come to understand: I could not stay in his home. It was too dangerous for us all. He had good reason to fear that the Germans would suspect him of hiding Jews again. But neither was Petro about to abandon me. He asked me to follow him into the woods. We walked in silence for several miles. When Petro felt we had ventured far enough, he began to dig a hole and filled it with straw and leaves. I made my way inside the hole and he covered me up. I was in hiding again.

Petro said, "Stay here. Don't come out. They're looking for you. I'll bring you food." It was cold and had snowed. I listened to Petro, and I stayed there no matter how miserable I got. It was terrible. I couldn't even relieve myself for long stretches of time. I couldn't do anything. My life was earth, mud, dirt, snow, straw, darkness and fear. I felt as if I had been buried alive.

I spent close to the entire winter in this hole. Petro would come to the hole and bring me food. Later on, I would risk climbing out of my grave and walking to Petro's house. I did this once every week or two. The walk was exhilarating; my muscles ached from staying still and thanked me for the chance to stretch. Petro gave me food and allowed me to stay there for a day or two before I turned back to my hole. Going from the coldness and filth of my hole to a warm home and back was like traveling between heaven and hell.

No sanctuary was entirely safe, not even my hidden hole. My safety was compromised around Christmas time of 1943. From within my covered hole I heard some Ukrainians in the forest. They had come to the woods to chop down trees for Christmas. I could do nothing but stay still until they disappeared. Later that night, while I was sleeping, a Ukrainian fell into the hole. I was stunned and terrified; I had been caught. Luckily, this Ukrainian and his friends were equally surprised by me. They all saw me, but they did not know that I was alone, and therefore their discovery frightened them enough to enable my escape.

Saved by a priest

I was desperate. Petro's house was far away, and I believed I was being chased. I crawled into the first barn I came across and hid with the cows. My hope was that I could pass two or three nights in this manner, until the discovery of my forest hiding place was old news. The owner of the barn was a terrible Ukrainian man. This was the reason I chose his barn; I imagined that no one would think to look for me there.

One morning, as he moved around straw for the cows, his pitchfork grabbed my feet. He was shocked to discover a Jew in his haystack and happy to see that he had hurt me. He pulled me out and attempted to stab me in the stomach with the pitchfork. All the while I was crying his name, screaming, "Don't kill me! Don't kill me!" Unable to finish the job on his own, the vicious farmer called out the whole village. I stood naked and bleeding as the villagers surrounded me, threatening me.

But they were not an angry mob. They were a gathering of people from the village conducting a town meeting of sorts, to decide what to do with me. There were different opinions.

"Cut out his tongue!" cried one.

"Cut off his head," said another.

"Cut off his feet," someone suggested.

A priest stepped out of the crowd. It was apparent that he had some standing in the community. He said, "Look, he's a child. He has lost everything. Let the Germans kill him, not us. Our reputations will be very bad if we kill the Jews, instead of letting the Germans kill him." The villagers listened to him. He came over to me and said, "We're not going to kill you today. Run to the Germans." I was crying and kissing him. I thanked him in Ukrainian. He told me, "God is with you." This priest saved my life.

Petro's last act

I arrived at Petro's doorstep for the very last time. Petro knew of the Ukrainian man who had stabbed me. He called him "the biggest no-good man." I needed Petro's advice. By that time he had been protecting me for a year and half. In many ways, he had become like a father to me. Few people would have done what he did for as long as he did it. Looking back on it, I am surprised he wasn't killed.

Petro said, "You know, the partisans are not far from here. I'm going to take you to them."

I had heard of the partisans before. They were members of a resistance movement that fought a guerrilla war against the occupation of the Soviet Union. Most important, as far as I was concerned, was the fact that they stood up to the Germans. The partisans he spoke of were situated about forty miles from Rastov. Most partisans typically lived in forests and had to overcome great obstacles to obtain food, shelter and weapons. Petro advised that I should seek shelter with them.

We didn't know if these particular partisans were Jewish or not. The Jewish partisans were made up of those who had escaped their ghettos and concentration camps. They were part of the underground Jewish Resistance Movement in Nazi Germany and would start ghetto uprisings and free Jewish prisoners. This movement rose out of the pure will to survive, and its members were willing to face the Nazi extermination machine, no matter what the odds. The Soviet partisans, however, were merely concerned with the guerrilla war waged against any occupying forces. Their mission was not the protection of the Jews, but fit Jewish men were usually welcomed by them. Either way, be it Jewish or Russian partisans, I had no choice now but to approach them in the hope that they would accept me into their ranks.

Petro agreed to walk me across German lines and make sure that I had been taken in. It was a dangerous trek, but as always our choice was between one danger and the other. I was resolute; it would be better than living in a hole, and I wouldn't be alone. The prospect of fighting back appealed to me as well. Petro and I walked all night until we came across a few partisans on horseback.

I eagerly explained to them all that I had been through and that I could fight. They asked me if I was a German. I told them, "No, I am a *Yevrei*, a Jew." At first they did not believe me and suspected me of being a German spy. I was asked to pull down my pants to prove my claim. I never imagined my *bris* would save my life. They were convinced.

It was time to bid farewell to Petro. His last words to me were fatherly. He said, "I hope they will take you in." I hugged him, and we cried. We didn't say much to each other, but I know we both understood that our bond was strong, and he knew how much I loved him. Petro passed away in 1974. His daughter, Nina, lives in Rastov to this day. I was fortunate enough to meet her again.

In 2008, Yad Vashem – The Holocaust Martyrs' and Heroes' Remembrance Authority, Jerusalem, recognized Mr. Petrivna Tokarsky as a Righteous Among the Nations, the honor bestowed upon non-Jews who saved Jews at great personal risk. Petro saved my life, and though he has since passed on, I will forever be in his debt.

The partisan general's girlfriend

I was on my own, but no longer alone. I followed the partisans to their camp in the woods. After months of living surrounded by enemies, it was truly a spectacular sight. The forest was alive with thousands of partisans, mostly men. As far as I could tell, there were no Jews there, and if there were, none of them were upfront about their religion. It didn't matter. They had taken me in.

The next thing I noticed was their weapons. I said to myself, "Oh my God." Each and every one of them had at least one weapon. These men were fighters. When I approached, I was immediately told, "We cannot take you in – you have to have your own gun." Another partisan, a very nice guy, gave me some helpful information: it seemed that the partisan general had a Jewish girlfriend.

I said, "How can I get to the girl?"

The partisan replied, "Come with me, I'll show you where the general with the Jewish girl lives."

He took me over to her. I came in to plead my case, and was crying before a word came out of my mouth. She was a beautiful girl, and she spoke to me in Yiddish, a language I hadn't heard in what seemed like an eternity. She told me, "I lost everything, and now I'm his girlfriend."

I said, "Can you take me in? Talk to your man; tell him to take me in with the partisans. I don't have a rifle, I don't have one and I don't know how to hold one, but I can learn if they give me one."

She looked at me with kind eyes and said, "I'll talk to him."

A partisan

She did as she promised, and soon enough the partisan general asked to speak to me. He said, "Tonight there are a lot of trains going to Stalingrad with German ammunition." The partisans had obtained information about a train that would be traveling nearby and carrying loads of German ammunition. The partisans had their mission: blow up the tracks and raid the ammunition. I was to join this raid.

They gave me a horse with a saddle, and taught me how to attach the explosives to the tracks properly. It was a large-scale mission, and its success depended on coordinating several hundreds of us. The train I was raiding was but one of many that night; it was a whole convoy. The Germans were having trouble in Stalingrad, and they urgently needed that ammunition.

When the train started coming towards us, I helped the partisans set explosives on the track and blow it up. The trains went up in the air and lit up the sky. This was a rush for me; I was finally getting a chance to hurt those who had hurt me, and even better, rob them of weapons they would have used to spread more death.

We raided the train, getting our hands on anything we could find that would protect us, including guns and ammunition we could carry away. This was exactly what the partisans were known for, and we were very lucky this time around. There were thousands and thousands of rifles for the taking. I ran over and took three rifles on my right shoulder, three rifles on my left shoulder and three on my back. The partisans saw me and said, "Very good!" Then I was one of them. I was given a basement to sleep in. I finally had a safe place to live and felt secure for the time being.

I remained with the partisans until early 1945. I learned that not all missions were as clean or successful as the first one I took part in. The Germans would retaliate. They attacked us and shot at us. They came with planes and bombed the woods we slept in. At night we'd go on missions. I was like a soldier. The chain of command was clear, and I followed orders. Partisans used to run to the farmers and take food. The partisans' existence was not easy, but I wasn't accustomed to having much food or to eating on a regular basis, so I didn't much mind these hardships. I was grateful for the chance to fight the Germans for two years.

The Jewish nurse

I was shot by the Germans on what was to be my final mission as a partisan. A horse and wagon took me and the other wounded to Sarny, a nearby *shtetl*. It was, of course, emptied of its former Jewish inhabitants, and the Russians had taken it over. I was sent to the home of a local farmer, to whom wounded partisans were often brought. A field hospital had been put together in the basement of his house. We lay on the floors; there were no beds. In addition to my gunshot wound, I had typhus, and I was sure that I was at death's door.

As the days went on, there seemed to be one nurse in particular who was always taking care of me. I decided to tell her I was Jewish. I can't say what brought me to confide in her, but something in my heart told me I needed to. She told me that she was Jewish as well. I shared my whole story with her, and it brought tears to her eyes. She said, "Don't say another word. I'm going to take you upstairs." There were better conditions up there.

From that day on she took care of me; she fed me and gave

me shots of antibiotics. These shots were meant only for the officers, but she had stolen some for my benefit. I felt better after that, and eventually I regained my health. I never saw her again. I wish I could have thanked her.

I was liberated by the Russians in January of 1945 in Sarny.

The Second World War had come to an end for me, though life had more hardships and miracles in store. My biggest miracle was my wife Rachel, whom I met a few months later. The next chapters of my life were no longer simply my own; I was able to share them with her…

RACHEL, RUNNING AND HIDING

Alone and on the run

That horrible night marked the end of my hometown Ozierany for the Jews, as well as the end of my father's life, but it was only the beginning of my nightmare. I was running. I was alone, bleeding and frightened. The sounds of death echoed around me. A young neighbor boy had run after me, convinced that my movement showed purpose and determination, that I knew where I was going and that I could save him. I was as unaware of his presence behind me as I was of where my legs were carrying me. I simply couldn't see him. In those moments of terror it seemed as if I was all alone in the world, just as I had been in my dream. Instead, this new reality was filled with people who would kill me on sight.

Unsure of where to go, I took a frantic risk. I headed toward a very dangerous place. A family that knew me well had a house near the railroad, which was swarming with Germans. I felt that no matter where I turned, I could not avoid their presence. My risk paid off, for a short while. My neighbor and I were both taken in by this family. The mother of the family washed me without a word. She didn't ask any questions, since she knew what had transpired over the night. Once I was clean, I felt almost normal again, warm and safe. Then she said, "You'll have to go, you can't stay here."

I didn't want to stay either, but I had to wait until it was dark again before I dared head out. The hours passed slowly, as they often did in hiding. The mother of this family had cleaned me, but I was still dirtying their home just by being there. As soon as the sun went down, my neighbor and I headed out to the railroad again, into danger. We split up at the railroad. I don't know where he went. I ducked into a barn and went into hiding.

Burning up in the barn

I was burning up with fever but was not aware of it. Between the terror and the rapid collapse of my world, I was incapable of distinguishing emotions and sensations from one another. I lay in the straw and shivered. And then I heard a voice, "Rochel, Rochel, are you here?" It was a friendly, loving voice, shouting in a careful whisper – my oldest brother Meyer. He had gone out in the night in search of his little sister and ran around looking for me until dawn. He risked his life, not for himself but for me.

I heard him calling out for me, yet I couldn't move or produce a sound to answer him. I was paralyzed by the fever, by the fear and by all that had befallen me. Finally the voice disappeared and all was quiet. I slept fitfully, never fully succumbing to it. Somehow, despite having nothing to eat or drink, I awoke the next day feeling that my strength had returned to me. My young body still had enough energy at this point to fight with all it had.

Once again, I waited for nightfall before moving. Luckily for me and my family, we had all agreed upon a rendezvous point in case it came to this. I managed to leave at night and make it to the place we had set up, overcome with relief to find them there, my dear brothers. All except Meyer were there. He was, of course, out looking for me and for our parents. We had no idea where our mother and father were.

After failing to find me in all of the places he'd imagined I would be, Meyer set off for Mizocz, a nearby village. He knew that a lot of people had gone there when fleeing the chaos of

Ozierany. Sure enough, Meyer found my mother in Mizocz. When he returned to our hiding place, we were overjoyed. My brothers were all alive.

Meyer said, "Let's all leave. You have to come with me and go to the ghetto in Mizocz. Our mother is there."

I cried when I heard that. I didn't want to go to another ghetto. Ghettos had one purpose in my mind and one possible ending. Even if it was safe for now, how long would it stay that way?

But Meyer was the oldest brother, and he insisted. "Rochel," he said, "Mama's there, we have to go."

Mizocz in flames

And so we walked to Mizocz. It was only two kilometers away, but it felt much further than that, as if we were marching to another land. None of us could feel at ease as long as we were out in the open, on the move, rather than safely hidden. But we made it, and my mother awaited us there with open arms. She hadn't seen any of her children except Meyer since the night she lost her husband. We all cried during that reunion. At first it seemed that Meyer had made the right decision for us: we were in another ghetto, but we were alive, and we were a family. That night I felt safe enough to fully fall asleep.

I was sleeping when the soldiers came. The doors burst open, and within an instant they were everywhere. They forced us out of the house. There was no place to run, but Meyer was not one to give up. Even as it was clear that there was no escape for us, he somehow set a few houses on fire in the hopes that it would provide a distraction and enable us to run. Or perhaps all he wanted was to make sure the Germans couldn't rob the houses. I have no idea how Meyer was able to set those fires, but it may have been thanks to the flames that one of my brothers, Zalman, was able to run away. For the rest of us, there were just too many of them. There were both German and Ukrainian policemen after us.

The only one of us who looked like a local Gentile was my brother Menachem. My mother had given him clothes to complete his look, and when he was spotted by the Ukrainians, who were usually very perceptive about who was and was not Jewish, they thought that he was one of them and that he was there to rob the Jewish houses. They asked him where he was from, and he named a Gentile place. They told him, "Please get out of here."

Poor Menachem didn't know what to do. He realized that the rest of us were being taken to our graves. We yelled to him, but of course we couldn't yell in German or Yiddish, since then his disguise would have been in vain. I don't know how he recognized what we were telling him, but he walked out. Menachem simply walked out of the ghetto. Zalman was already out. I remained with Meyer, Yossel and my mother. We had been captured, and it seemed all was over for us.

Walk of death

They marched us out to be killed. As we walked, images were seared into my mind. We passed the house of Shulem, the barber who had hidden me for three weeks. Shulem was lying in a pool of blood with his guts torn out of his body. I saw an elderly man. He was doing his best to keep up with the march, but his age held him back. He couldn't walk well enough, so they shot him on the spot and kept moving. They didn't wait for him to die; they left him there to die on the ground.

It seemed impossible that we should pass by these atrocities and keep on walking, but that was what we did. It was daytime by then, and the sun was shining down on us. I talked to God. I asked him, "How can you let people die on such a beautiful day?" There was nobody there to listen to me. Everybody around me was choked with fear, their throats tightened, letting go only to sound screams and sobs.

And curses. Someone was cursing in Ukrainian. I looked up and I saw that the cursing was coming from the lips of a Ukrainian policeman. I hadn't been aware of the fact that he had been cursing at me. When he'd gotten my attention, he said under his breath, "Go over to the right side." I had been walking on the left side, which was blocked by a sugar factory, so there was no way anybody could run away through there. On the right side there was a little hill and a few scattered houses.

Once I'd made it to the other side, doing nothing more than following this man's gruff orders, the Ukrainian policeman said, "I'm going to shoot in the air. Don't look back – just run."

I didn't have the time to comprehend what was going on, that this enemy soldier was saving my life. He did as he said he would and shot into the air. Gunfire was not a strange sound to be heard on that death march, so it drew little attention. For me it was like a starter's pistol. I shot off with the bullet. This time I could tell that I wasn't alone: my brother Yossel ran after me, a neighbor boy ran and another little boy I had never met before all ran after me, all hoping for the same – to live. My mother and my brother Meyer tried to run as well, but other soldiers turned them back, and they returned to the line.

The four of us – Yossel, my neighbor, the little boy and I – were all running. We heard somebody running after us, but we didn't dare look back. The soldiers couldn't tell for sure how many children they were chasing, and that was our luck. The Ukrainian people saw us running, but they didn't do anything. They stood by as we ran for our lives.

In those days, toilets were rarely inside the houses. Instead there were little outhouses in the yards. We ran into one of these and hid between toilets. The little boy who had joined us nearly choked me to death; he was so frightened that he pushed and pushed at me even though there was nowhere for me to go. The soldiers shot at us, and one of their bullets hit the little boy.

He screamed out and ran away from the outhouse, crying. I don't know what happened to him after that. I imagine he was killed. I believe that the soldier who'd shot him had only seen the little boy, and after he'd killed him, he thought it was over. The rest of us were left alone. The soldiers didn't know we were there.

Children on their own

Once we were convinced that no one was waiting for us on the outside, my brother Yossel, the neighbor boy and I left the toilets and ran out to the fields. As we ran, I remember passing by little Gentile girls who were sitting and cleaning white beets for sugar. I envied those girls. For them, nothing had happened. Life was the same, and it was beautiful.

We ran until we could run no more, and then the three of us sat down. We looked on toward the railway. Once again I had reached a very dangerous area, the only place I could think to run. German and Ukrainian policemen were not the only danger to be found at the railroad tracks; there were also a lot of bandits there. They killed the Jews as well. We remained at a distance, too afraid to get close and be killed by them.

We saw a German riding the railroad on a small motorized vehicle. He was coming toward us, but luck was on our side at that moment. This man was the same German who had helped my brother get me out of work. My brother had told me that this German was a very good-hearted man who didn't like what was being done to the Jews. I started yelling, and he immediately stopped and picked us all up. His presence made me feel protected, that I was meant to live.

He wanted to take us to somebody who would shelter us, but I said, "No, thank you." We let him drive us closer to my family's old rendezvous point, and there we bid him farewell. He was not happy that we, just children, would continue running around and risking our lives, but he could only offer his assistance. He could not and would not force us to stay. We got off and started to run.

This time the rendezvous spot held tragedy and miracle alike. Menachem and Zalman had made it there and were waiting for us; they had escaped, as well. Meyer and my mother never came back. Within a few days I had lost my father, and now my mother and my older brother. I was the eldest survivor of our family, and in that moment I became mother, father and older sister for all the others. My three brothers were now my children. I had saved the neighbor boy's life. Without me he never would have run, since he didn't know where to go or what to do. He trusted me and followed everything I told him. I wished I had someone to tell me what to do.

Death in a dream

We lived in hiding behind the house of a Czech man we knew. He had a large stack of straw outside, and we made a hole in it and crawled inside. We covered up the opening with straw, and this was our home. We lived like rats, and we ate like rats as well. If we had only one meal a day and if it was just a piece of bread, it was enough. Since we didn't want anybody to know where we were, or that we were even together, we split up the nights of the week among ourselves. One of us would go out each night to find food and then remained in hiding during the other nights until his or her turn came round again. This was how we lived; we were either in hiding or out begging for bread.

On one of these nights I had another dream so real, I knew I could not ignore it. In it I was clearly warned not to allow my brother Zalman to go out for bread, because if I did, he would surely get killed. I woke up in a sweat and shook my brothers. I said, "Remember, I had a dream. Don't forget to remind me not to let Zalman go out. Please remind me!" But nobody remembered, not even myself. A bad dream easily got lost in the shuffle when waking life was a nightmare. My brother Zalman's turn came around, and he went out and never came back.

There was another Czech man living nearby whom I had always avoided. I never went over there begging for bread. I didn't like him. His parents had been nice, but he was a terrible person. He befriended Hungarian soldiers. My dear brother Zalman didn't know any better. He came there looking for food, for a bit of kindness, and they immediately took him out and shot him. He never even got to have his Bar Mitzvah, and he never received a proper funeral, either. We don't know where he's buried.

Our family was now only the three of us: Menachem, Yossel and I. We grieved for the loss of our parents and brothers, but there was nothing we could do. We couldn't visit their graves, and my brothers couldn't say the Kaddish over them with the necessary *minyan* [prayer quorum of ten Jewish men]. We honored their deaths by hanging on to our lives, remaining in hiding for many months to come. When word of liberation came, it was a joy marred with sadness. We headed out for the nearby city of Rowne, where I would meet my husband Sam, and where our stories would finally merge.

SAM AND RACHEL, LIBERATION

Off to Rowne (Rivne)

After I was nursed back to health and liberated from the Germans, I found myself healthy, free and lost. My entire life as a young man had been comprised of running, hiding and fighting. After all that, at the age of nineteen, I was left to ask, "What am I going to do now?"

I had made up my mind not to return to the partisans. I had served them well and suffered a war injury. Word went out that the Russian army was not too far off from Rowne, and I decided I would head there in search of my fate.

I stood at the side of the road and tried to hail the Russian soldiers who were also going to Rowne. One of these soldiers was kind enough to tell me he was driving there in his truck, and I gladly joined him. When we arrived at Rowne, he said to me, "The Poles are going to put together an army, and they're going to fight for Warsaw. In Rowne, maybe they'll take you in to join the fight." I had arrived without any prospects, and the Polish army seemed as good as any. However, it wasn't to be. The Polish army would not accept me, but in hindsight, I was probably lucky they turned me down.

Rowne had been liberated by the Russians. Russian soldiers were there, and we were safe, but at nighttime the Germans would still spitefully shoot bullets from their losing side. I had nowhere to turn, and so I made my bed in a remote ditch. I dug a hole and hid in it. Maybe this was force of habit. That evening, from my hiding place I heard the sounds of soldiers passing by. Hearing Russian, I was drawn to peek out of my hiding place. The Russian soldiers, alarmed that I might be a German, grabbed me by the hair and pulled me out.

As soon as they got a good look at me, their behavior changed. One of the soldiers said, "My child, you're barefoot and half-naked. It's sixty-four below outside!" He seemed to be a kind man, and I begged him to help me. I had no family left and no place to go. During desperate moments like these, I often spoke to my mother. I had survived, yet I had still not fulfilled her final wish that I would tell my tale and all that I had seen. I cried out to her that I had no one to speak to – "Mama, to whom can I tell my story?"

Caught up in emotions, I was unaware that I had said these words aloud. As soon as he recognized my Yiddish, the Russian soldier demanded to know what I was saying.

"I'm speaking to my mother," I replied. I didn't care how this sounded.

The Russian surprised me. He said, "I'm Jewish too."

He was a complete stranger, but I hugged him tightly. I don't know what came over me. After surviving alone all those years, without a family, without a place in the world, I craved some humanity. A look of kindness on the face of a fellow Jew was enough. I said, "Please, help me. What should I do?"

He said, "My child, you're barefoot. The snow is high, and you don't have any clothes on. Let me go and get some rags and put them around your feet, and I'll take you to the synagogue."

A mother in Rowne

Months of hiding passed before we were sure that it was safe to move. When we believed we could emerge back into the world, my family's three survivors, Menachem, Yossel and I, set out for the recently liberated city of Rowne. Many Jewish survivors had arrived there before us, and we got to know the small survivor community. Among these survivors was Moshka, my mother's first cousin. Just as we had taken on small orphaned children, Moshka lived with a little girl who was seven or eight years old. He had helped her survive. We were overjoyed to encounter a living relative, but this joy did not last long.

Even after liberation, life remained perilous. Antisemitism did not abide by the rules of war; its roots were deep and its dangers remained palpable for many years to come. Despite being free we were still destitute, forced to go out begging for necessities, so Moshka left the little girl in my care and went out to the Gentiles to ask for food. He never came back. The Nazis had been defeated and run out of Rowne, but it seemed the locals didn't need their racist guidance. He was killed by Ukrainians for being a Jew; choked to death in the street. The little girl was left with me.

Other children flocked to me, and I continued my role as a surrogate mother. I was responsible for several children, boys and girls of different ages. As the oldest, I was not only mother but also teacher. There were three little girls that I taught every day. Barely a young adult myself, I was now preoccupied with the daily concerns of adulthood: providing food, shelter and care for those younger than me. Yet when it came to love, I was as much of a child as those I had taken under my wing. I was as naïve about boys and romance as a little girl, and I certainly was not prepared to meet my future husband.

The girl in the synagogue

As he had promised, the Russian soldier led me to the synagogue in Rowne. He told me that many survivors had gathered there. There had been a bustling community of 30,000 Jews in Rowne before the Holocaust, so it was a big synagogue. Liberated Jews had all gathered in the synagogue, which had become a makeshift center for them. I walked excitedly through the snow with barely a rag to my feet. The Russian soldier was amazed.

"How is it possible for you to walk barefoot in the snow like this?" he asked.

I said, "I have been walking like this for five years."

The Russian soldier brought me up to the building. I thanked him, and we parted. It was nighttime, and I had no clear idea of where I was. I found my way inside and realized I was standing amongst horses. The horses kicked me and urinated on me. A fear crept up, that I had been misled and brought to the wrong place. Suddenly I heard people speaking Yiddish. It was like music to my ears. The voices were coming through the wall, from the other side. Then I understood; the Germans had split this holy place in half and allotted one half for the horses and the other half for their own purposes. Liberation had been too recent to rectify this.

I knocked on the door of the synagogue, and my future wife came to the door. She looked very young. Her clothes were tattered. She said in Yiddish, "What do you want?"

I said, "Take me in." I grabbed her by the hand and said, "*Mameh, mameh.*"

She said, "I'm not your mother. What do you want from me? Don't call me '*mameh*'."

Yet she took me in. What I saw inside that synagogue seemed like heaven. Anybody else would have seen a ragged bunch huddled around watery soup made of rotten potatoes and whatever else they were able to scrounge up. To my eyes they were beautiful people enjoying a feast.

I begged her for food. She said, "You just came in. There are many people waiting to be served ahead of you." Nevertheless, she gave me a bowl of soup, which I ate within seconds. People gathered around me and asked me how I had found this place, and I told them that the Russian soldier had brought me. He was yet another angel whose name I did not know.

There were older people in the synagogue, along with young people like Rachel and little boys and girls. About thirty or forty people were living there. The Russians were kind enough to bring us bread. Rachel was responsible for of many of the children. She would run out to the market every day, and when the farmers threw away rotten fruit and vegetables she took a bucket and collected them for her soup. Before Passover she ran out and made matzo. Looking back on it now, I believe I loved her from the first moment I laid eyes on her.

Lost papers and a prophecy

Food was scarce in liberated Rowne. Not only was getting a proper job difficult, but movement was quite limited between cities and villages. A special permit was needed from the Russians for traveling from place to place. Luckily, I was able to obtain permission in paper; otherwise it's hard to say what I would have done for food.

I followed in my father's footsteps and became a traveling saleswoman. I bought fifty kilos of white flour with what little money I had. With this flour in hand, I headed off to Kiev. I carried the fifty-kilo sack myself, though if you asked me how I did it, I could not explain it. It's hard for me to believe I was able to carry that much with me, yet I know I did. I had to. Not only was I able to carry the flour, but when I passed through the checkpoints and presented my papers, I was able to push it along without the Russian soldiers noticing it.

In Kiev, I avoided the market and went straight to the black market. I'd become acquainted with a special spot where I would meet the buyer. Then, with the money I would make from selling the flour, I would purchase things such as needles and thread, merchandise that was unavailable in Rowne but also not heavy and therefore would not cause me much trouble.

Back in Rowne, somebody came and bought this merchandise from me. I didn't like going to the market and dealing with buyers in the open. Every trip allowed me to stay at home in Rowne with the kids for two weeks, and when the money ran out I left enough food for the children to eat during my absence, and set out for Kiev once again.

I didn't have a purse to hold my permit papers in, so I stashed them in my pocket. On one of these sales trips, after crossing over into Kiev, I put my hand into my pocket and discovered that my papers were gone. I felt stranded. I was away from all the children who were dependent on me, and the Russians would surely arrest me when they found out I was without papers. Fear took hold of me and slowed me down; I did everything I had to do as if underwater. Walking through the streets with my new merchandise in hand, I passed by a blind fortuneteller and decided to hear her out. She took my hand in hers and ran her fingers over it in an intense concentration. Her head bobbed back and forth.

Finally she spoke. "You have to go a long way, and you're afraid. You lost something very precious, and you're afraid to go back. But don't be afraid; you'll get home. You will get wherever you're going." She took my other hand, squeezed it and studied it with her fingers. "You'll have a long life... you will marry a nice man... you'll have three children... you will be rich. You'll have a very interesting life."

Though I had not decided whether I believed her or not, the fortuneteller's words comforted me. As I sat in the train to go home, however, I found I was shaking. I looked out the window, expecting nothing, and suddenly I saw my uncle Mendel walking alongside the train. He boarded the same train I was on. I walked up to his window, knocked and waved. He recognized me in disbelief, and we rejoiced. He had not been the best uncle I could have hoped for, but he was family, and with his help I was able to return along with him and his own family to my children in Rowne.

The Secret Police

After settling in and regaining my humanity in Rowne, I got a good job with Russian intelligence. People knew of a Jewish officer who held a position within their ranks, and they said, "Go over there and see if he'll help you." I went and spoke with him. He was a very nice man who was interested in my story and in helping me out. He said, "I'll send you to Kiev for a few months, and they'll teach you."

I went off to Kiev on my own to undergo training. My previous meeting with Rachel had been brief, and I had no idea that she would become my wife, let alone that there was reason to stay in Rowne on her account. When I was done, I was officially a part of the Russian NKVD, the secret police.

Over the years, the NKVD undertook many operations ranging from regular policing in Russia to execution, forced labor, purges and assassinations. My place in the NKVD was solely within their operations in the liberated parts of Ukraine, dealing with Ukrainians who had collaborated with the Nazis. The Russians didn't speak Ukrainian, and they needed our help in picking up Ukrainians and putting them in jail. They were after Ukrainian collaborators and bandits. We could speak their language and, in many cases, identify those who had sided with the Nazis. We were able to do to these Ukrainians what they had so brutally done to us, their former peaceful neighbors.

We took a truck and head into the country to arrest them. During these missions, I looked all over for the black-hearted Ukrainian who had tried to kill me with his pitchfork, but I couldn't find him. I did pick up a few Ukrainians that I knew had killed people. We brought them into the city so that all could see them. Our operations were risky, and we all feared we would get caught and be sent to Siberia, but we felt that justice was being served. I was a proud, well-respected officer.

During this time I went to Turzysk as well, which was also a risk. I was giving hope one last chance. Maybe, somehow, someone had survived after all – a sister, an uncle, a familiar face. There were no Jews left in Turzysk when I arrived. The year was 1945. I met some Gentiles who had known me. My presence shocked them. "You're alive!" they cried, "We saw you walking to the grave!"

The visit was worthwhile for one reason: I got to see Petro one last time. He couldn't believe I was alive. It brings me great joy to this day that I was able to see him and show him that his efforts had been worthwhile – I had survived. Afterwards I walked around my old hometown and felt surrounded by ghosts. At the graveside of the Turzysk Tzaddik, I let loose my tears. A Ukrainian man walked over to me and offered a kind word of warning, "Don't stay here. It's going to be dark; they're going to kill you here." I went away and stayed away for many years to come. I returned to Rowne, in uniform.

Found papers and a husband-to-be

We had no running water, and so one of my many duties was to fetch two bucketsful. The Russian soldiers were still a source of fear and concern for me. Though I had made it back without my papers, I felt I was still in danger. If I was headed to the shop, I always crept out the back way, but when I brought back water, I had no choice but to come in through the front. I walked up the street for all to see, carrying two buckets overflowing with water.

One day, a man came out of the blue and took the buckets from me. He was not a thief; he simply helped me to my house. However, I was still afraid of him because he wore a Russian uniform. This man, who helped me in silence, turned out to be a friend of Sam's.

Sam's friend always came out of nowhere. He was a little older, and he looked after Sam like a son. His appearance was Jewish, and so I asked if he was. He replied, joking, "I'm a *Yiddishe goy*," meaning, "I'm a 'Jewish Gentile.'" He decided I would be good for Sam and told him, "Come with me, I'll take you to see a nice Jewish girl."

One Sunday, Sam came upstairs. He was wearing a Russian army uniform, like his friend. His sudden appearance scared me. I was worried to death. Three of my cousins, young girls, were up there with me, as well as three other girls who sat in another corner. Sam looked straight at me and asked me, "Would you like to come with me to a movie?"

I said, "No, thank you."

But Sam was not deterred. He kept coming to see me, so I

decided to disappear. I instructed the children to keep everything from him. I said, "When that soldier comes, he's going to ask where I am, and you're going to say you don't know." I didn't trust him. Men frightened me, and I didn't want any man around me. This was a fear I had carried with me from the hiding place, and for a while it felt like it would never go away. While I was afraid, Sam wasn't. He fell in love with me right away. All I knew was that I didn't want any part of it. If he came across me, he'd ask me where I'd been, and I'd say "Don't ask me. It's none of your business."

One day, I came home and the children told me that a Russian soldier had been at the house looking for me. Of course, I believed it was Sam. I asked, "Did he say anything?" The children surprised me. The soldier had not said anything but to meet him at the soldiers' headquarters. I realized it was not Sam. I knew what that visit had been about. I'd lost my papers, and now they'd found them.

I very well may have been walking straight into a prison sentence or worse, but I walked into the headquarters with my head held high. "Did you find my papers?" I asked. The Russian soldier I spoke to was so surprised that for a moment I was sure he was going to keel over. They were shocked that I knew why they'd called me in. Once they got over their surprise, they tried to interrogate me. "Did you give your papers to the bandits?" They demanded to know.

I said, "No! How can you even accuse me of that kind of thing? I'm Jewish, and they kill Jews."

The soldier wasn't sure how to respond to that.

"How did you lose them?" he finally asked.

"How do you lose something?" I said. "I had a pocket, and they fell out. I have no purse."

He had no choice but to return my papers. As he did, he warned me, "Be careful. Don't lose them this time."

Apparently I had lost them on the way to Kiev. Had they been found past the checkpoint, I would not have gotten off so easily.

The parachutes

Sam was not as easy to get rid of as those Russian soldiers. He bothered me so much one evening I felt as if I were going to die. Since I had adamantly refused to go to the movies with him, he offered me to work with him during the winter. It was getting too hard to say no.

During this time, Sam thought nothing but good things about his friend, the older Russian man who had brought us together. I realized then that the reason the man always seemed to come out of nowhere was that one block further down from my house lived a group of partisans. It was a house of heavy drinking, mostly vodka. I knew nothing about drinking, but I had a feeling there was something about this man I did not like.

Sam was nothing like those partisans; he stayed away from alcohol and concerned himself with my well-being. Clothes were as scarce as food at the time, and when Sam saw that I had a tattered jacket but no material to sew it up with, he told me that he and this friend had access to parachutes at their workplace. Parachutes are made from a beautiful, strong material. Sam used to give all this material away to his friend, believing he himself had no use for it.

I asked Sam, "You're giving it to him? Why?"

He said, "What should I do with it?"

I said, "You're endangering your life and you're not even keeping any of the spoils for yourself? At least keep it for yourself and sell it." I knew that his Russian friend didn't need it; he was happy with a bottle of whiskey.

Sam's friend loved me to death, but when I told Sam not to give the parachute away — that if his friend wanted to have it, he could buy Sam's half from him — he said to Sam, "Now you're listening to that girl? She's stupid!"

My little brother Yossel came to my defense. He came up to Sam's friend and declared, "Don't you dare come to this house, and don't you dare talk about my sister. She's not dumb. She's smart. She's a nice girl, and she's beautiful." The man stayed away from our house, but continued to try and make me look ugly in Sam's eyes. He didn't understand that Sam was already in love and deaf to his words.

Grab the suitcase and run

The money that I didn't spend on necessities for myself and the children was stashed away in a wooden suitcase. I was always cautious with money, saving up for a rainy day. My intent was to cash it in for gold coins. Our rainy day happened to be a nice summer day. I had a little balcony, and I was sitting out there with the suitcase when I saw Sam running toward our house. He cried out to me from the street, "We have to run away!"

I said, "What are you talking about?"

He ran up and explained. His friend and partner in their illegal black market peddling had been caught, and now the Russians were looking for him. I had to go with him because he had a picture of me in his apartment, and his friend had told the Russians where they lived. The soldiers could easily find my picture there, and so, just in case they did, I had to run.

I told the children to stay put. The Russian soldiers were not going to touch the children. I didn't leave the children a penny, but there was plenty of food in the house. I told them I was going to run away to Dubno and from there to Luck. The children were to follow and meet up with us in Dubno.

Yossel said he would be there, but my little cousin said she wasn't going. She preferred to join the Haganah. The Haganah was the Jewish paramilitary underground organization that grew up in Eretz Israel-Palestine and became the core of the Israeli Defense Forces. In liberated areas, the Haganah took in young people without families and eventually brought them to Israel.

As Sam and I walked down the street in Dubno, I saw Russian soldiers, high-ranking officers. I said under my breath, "Sam, hide yourself. If they only see me, we'll be fine." Unfortunately, Sam didn't listen to me. They arrested us both and took us to Luck. If

Sam hadn't talked to them, everything would have been fine, but Sam had too much faith in the Russians.

They took Sam and me over to their station, where they asked us questions. They wouldn't let us talk to each other; they kept us separate. I saw Sam through a window. A couple of officers who knew Sam came in. When they saw him, they all hugged. They asked, "What are you doing here?" I wasn't supposed to be listening in on them, let alone speaking to them, but I kept saying, in Yiddish, "Go with them!"

I whispered to him through the window that he should walk back to Dubno on their tails, and this time he listened to me. He didn't want to go, but I said, "You go. What will they hold me for? What did I do? Go!" Nobody touched Sam because everybody thought that he was with the soldiers who had just walked in. It was already nightfall, and he made it out by doing simply that, walking behind these men. They knew him, they talked to him, but they had no idea that he was sticking with them in order to escape.

I was left alone. Finally the interrogators returned. They immediately bombarded me with questions about Sam's disappearance. I said, "How should I know where he went?" One of the interrogators insisted, "You have pictures with him." I said, "Haven't you ever taken a picture when you saw a pretty girl?" After all I had been through, I wasn't afraid of these people. But they didn't like what I was saying, or perhaps the way I had been saying it. They put me in a dark room and locked me up for the night.

From Dubno to Chelm

I remained in that room until sunrise. It was windowless and bare; they hadn't even left me a chair to sit on. I spent the night on the floor, in complete darkness. It was only when the door was opened that I saw the sun had come up. I was taken out of the room and brought to another interrogator. They started questioning me, and I interrupted them, "You're the liberators?" I asked, "You're worse than Hitler. You put me in a dark room with nowhere to sit?"

I yelled and yelled at them. I think the Russian soldier was either Jewish himself or knew some Jews and liked them because my words affected him. He said, "Please, don't be mad. You can go."

I went back to Dubno. There was a Ukrainian Communist who lived there named Ivan, who was our friend. When I got to his place, Yossel was already there waiting for me, and, of course, Sam had arrived as well. I told Ivan that we wished to go to Poland, because from Poland we would be able to go to so many places, while from Dubno we couldn't really get anywhere. My uncle Mendel and his family had gone to Poland for this reason as well. He had been afraid to stay and so he'd run away from the Russians, and now he would be there to take us in when we arrived.

Ivan agreed to help us. He said, "I have a cousin who was taken by the Russian army. I don't know if he's alive or dead. Why don't you give Sam my cousin's papers, and if he runs into any problems, he can show the papers to the authorities."

We left Dubno hidden in the back of a wagon. We covered ourselves up with straw and rode close to the railroad tracks. When the train started moving, we shook off the straw and jumped onto it. We jumped off the train when it arrived at Chelm, which was the closest stop. This was a train that kept going back and forth to pick up things, and so it didn't go very far in either direction, and they never bothered to close the doors. That was how we reached Poland.

In Chelm

Rachel and I had run away together. We weren't married yet, but I think we both understood that we had become a couple, for better or for worse. Separation was not an option. After our experience in Dubno and Luck, Rachel understood that my dealings put me in constant danger of being sent to jail. If I was at risk, so was she. It was a transient way of living; our goal was to reach *Eretz Israel*, then Mandatory Palestine. We hoped to make our way from Poland to Czechoslovakia and from there to England and finally Palestine.

We made our temporary home in Chelm. We stayed with Rachel's uncle, Mendel, and used the time to save up some money and make the right connections. The Polish black market was the only employment I could find, though it was not without its dangers. After the war, there were still pogroms. Jews were still being murdered, and Chelm was subject to this violence as well. We were afraid of being killed.

I used to go out and sell something, anything, as long as I got something for us to eat in return. On one of these occasions I was in the market, trying to sell off whatever small merchandise I had acquired, and the antisemitic Poles came out at me with a stick, intent on beating me to death. I ran away, sad and horrified. It was clear that as long as we remained in Poland, we would remain hunted and haunted.

Later on, I met another Turzysk survivor, a man by the name of Meyer. We struck up a partnership, went to Katowice and bought clothing there, then came back to Chelm and sold it off for a marginal profit. I made enough money this way to support Rachel and her little brother Yossel, and later on it sufficed to buy what little was needed for our modest wedding.

The chicken

It was in Chelm that we finally decided we were going to get married. Ours was to be the first Jewish marriage there. Our marriage was as much the wish of the Jewish survivors surrounding us as a fulfillment of our own desires. They kept saying, "You know, you're two nice kids. You should get married." I didn't know what marriage meant. And neither did Rachel. We had never really thought about it, but our neighbors were adamant and so excited.

It got so that people approached us and pleaded for our engagement. I recall one man who said to me, "Please, I'm going to help you. We want to have a married couple. We want to start Jewish life anew, to show Hitler that he didn't succeed." Others agreed. They said, "We're going to show Hitler. We're the first ones liberated and we're going to have the first Jewish wedding!" This wedding was a symbol for them, a show of strength and an act of hope.

Everybody told us we had to get married, and we believed them. Rachel came from a very religious family. She said to me, "We have to have a chicken for the wedding." A chicken was harder to come by at that time, and it would have been out of our price range. However, everybody was quick to lend me a few pennies, and I went out to the market and got a chicken. Now all we needed was a *shochet* to kill the chicken, but they knew of no one.

A volunteer stepped forward proudly. He said, "In Lublin, my grandfather was a *shochet*, and I used to watch him. I know how to do it." He went over to the chicken with a knife, but he wasn't able to cut all the way through. He had barely wounded the chicken, and the panicked bird managed to flap its wings so frantically that he was forced to let go. The chicken flew away. I was crying, and the poor guy was crying too. It seemed like the worst thing that could have happened.

I came back to Rachel with my head hung low. Rachel asked, "Where's the chicken?"

I said, "The chicken flew away."

The others did not hesitate. "We're still going through with the wedding," they said.

The wedding

Among the people liberated after the war, weddings happened quickly. As soon as a couple liked each other, they got married. Two of my cousins, my Uncle Mendel's daughters, were already married. One of them lived far away from Chelm, in Lodz. The other cousin, Pola, had married and then moved with her husband to Chelm, along with her father.

I went to visit Pola to get a glimpse of young married life. When I walked in, I found them both in bed. In my eyes, Pola was a child, and her husband looked like my grandpa. She was Uncle Mendel's youngest one, only a little bit older than my brother

Yossel. I couldn't understand what those two had in common that had led them to get married. I knew I wouldn't have been able to touch an older man.

Sam was my age, and he was good looking, but my uncle didn't like him. Though he had no reason to dislike him, Mendel and my Aunt Toby still made Sam's life difficult. One day Toby and Mendel talked to Sam in such foul language that it hurt me more than it had hurt Sam. That day he and I decided we were going to get married. I think I got married because I couldn't hurt Sam any more. My aunt and uncle constantly insulted him, and he deserved much better.

We came in to my uncle's living room and announced that we'd decided to get married. My aunt's first thought was that I'd gotten pregnant. How she could have thought something like that, I don't know. I wouldn't even let Sam kiss me before we were married. It goes to show how little my aunt and uncle understood about me, my values and my character.

Upon hearing the news, my brother Yossel couldn't stop crying. He cried because his sister was to be married, and he had no parents and no brothers with him. I think he was afraid that I wouldn't love him anymore. He was very disappointed and emotional. Toby and Mendel did little to hide their lack of excitement concerning our wedding, yet all the other Jewish survivors who lived in Chelm were happy and supportive. Everyone came to the wedding – they all came running.

A couple with children from my hometown of Ozierany had also survived. The woman's wedding dress had somehow survived, too, and she offered to bring me the wedding dress for my ceremony. I only had a dark blue house-dress, but I decided that this was what I was going to get married in. It felt like the right thing. I thanked the girl but refused to take her dress. Sam wore somebody's jacket, and I wore a light scarf on my head.

We didn't have any food to eat on our wedding day. Instead, we fasted until the ceremony. When Sam returned without a chicken, our wedding guests ran to the Poles and Ukrainians and returned with some bread. We had ten men as witnesses, forming a *minyan*. We didn't know any of these ten people. One of them wore a white shirt. He gladly tore it up for us, and they made a *huppah* out of it – a marriage canopy to stand underneath for the ceremony.

We didn't have a rabbi, but religious people were present, and they wrote up the *ketubah*, the Jewish marriage contract, in Yiddish. When they saw my signature, Rochel Czerkiewicz, they all were very happy that I had learned to write Hebrew in a *cheder*. I didn't have to mention the *cheder*; they saw my handwriting and understood. There were no pictures taken, but I remember the event clearly. That's the way I got married. I still have my marriage license with me, to this day.

Married

Rachel and I were both very naïve. The war had shaped our lives in such a way that some of the most elementary aspects of the relationship between men and women were unknown to us. We were on our way to becoming parents without knowing how children were brought into the world. We didn't know what marriage truly was, or that we were meant to sleep together on our wedding night. After the *huppah*, we each went to sleep in our separate beds. We simply didn't know what we were supposed to do.

In the following days, all those who had been urging us to get married now changed their tune to, "You have to have a baby." We didn't know how that was done. One lady offered to take us in and give us the talk about the "facts of life." Despite that, when it finally happened, we were not prepared for it; we didn't know about the signs of pregnancy. There was no doctor back then, and there were no hospitals, and so when Rachel became pregnant, she didn't know about it for five or six months.

Married

I didn't know what we were supposed to do after we got married. On my wedding night we slept together in the same room with my family; we weren't alone, Sam and I, and we slept in separate beds. In the morning, when I woke up, I sat with Sam and saw my aunt snooping around my bed. At the time, I didn't know what she was looking for.

Years later, it came to me: she wanted to know if I was still a virgin or not. But nothing had happened during that night. I was ashamed. I didn't even let him kiss me. I was brought up in a house with four brothers, and we had never talked about things like that. I had nobody to ask questions. And then I was alone. Whom would I have asked? Sam and I were left to discover everything on our own...

PART II: AMERICA

SAM AND RACHEL, AMERICA

Förenwald

Rachel and I had gotten married, but life had not yet changed for us. Chelm was not where we wanted to be, and we'd wound up staying there much longer than we had planned to. Now that we were a married couple and soon to be a family, the squalid life Chelm offered us as impoverished, illegal, ever-hunted Jews became unacceptable. Finally I said it out loud, "How long can we stay like this?"

Through my dealings, I met a Russian officer. I asked him, "Can you take us over to the border?"

He set us on our path. The journey to the American Zone in Munich was a treacherous one, though after all we had been through, something about it was almost natural. We had to climb mountains like antelopes and crawl on the ground like snakes, arriving unseen in the middle of the night, but none of this was new to either of us. My mother's words, *"Run, don't look back,"* guided me once again. It was a night that I would remember for many years to come, though it was thankfully uneventful. Behind those mountains was a better future, possibly in Palestine, and that was our ultimate goal. Rachel and I were taking our lives in our own hands, and it felt right.

Once we made it across the border we were taken over to a DP (Displaced Persons) camp named Förenwald. Houses that had once been populated by SS officers and soldiers of the Gestapo were now, in a welcome twist of irony, given to refugees like ourselves, most of whom had been persecuted by the Nazis, and many of whom were Jewish. We were given tiny rooms, to be shared by two or three couples together. We were fed there and allowed to grow.

From 1946 to 1948, Förenwald grew to become the third largest DP camp in the American sector, after Feldafing and Landsberg. The camp's initial population was comprised of Jewish, Yugoslavian, Hungarian and Baltic refugees. On October 3, 1945, General Dwight D. Eisenhower ordered that Förenwald be made an exclusively Jewish DP camp, after finding the living conditions at the Feldafing camp unacceptable. By January 1946, Förenwald's population had grown from 3,000 to 5,300. Many couples got married there, following the same urge that our neighbors in Chelm had voiced to us: the desire to rebuild and rise from the ashes. The birth rate in Förenwald in 1946 was rapid, with approximately 200 women pregnant at the same time.

We spent four years in Förenwald, waiting for an opportunity to arise. Rachel gave birth to our first son, Steve, in that camp. He was born in our little apartment, with the help of a midwife.

Though the camp was big, I had no one to whom I could tell my story. My best friend was my wife, Rachel. As we talked and learned about the paths that had led us together, we grew closer to each other. Our dreams were one and the same.

Steve

We wanted to go to Palestine. I was already four months pregnant, but I didn't know that. The changes my body was going through were a mystery to me, and I assumed, as those around me did, that I had fallen ill. Though I was pregnant, I was malnourished and skinny. Convinced that I was sick, I lost my appetite and brought the weight loss upon myself.

During those nine months I ate potatoes with the skin and rye bread with nothing on it, and I drank tea. For the most part, that was it. Any time I had a craving, Sam was quick to bring me whatever I needed. Sam found me anything I wanted, even things that were rare and hard to get at the time, like oranges, and brought them to me. He had connections at the camp and was making whiskey in our basement.

There were many boys in the DP camp, friends of ours, who were very obvious about the fact that they were attracted to me. I had been so healthy and pretty when I'd arrived there, and all of a sudden I was lying in bed. The boys from the camp used to come over to our apartment, and when they saw my condition, they wanted to kill Sam. They thought he wasn't taking care of me. Perhaps they secretly hoped that was true, so that one of them could take his place.

One day I mustered up the strength to leave the apartment for a breath of fresh air. My neighbor saw me, and she was the one who suggested that maybe I was pregnant. I didn't say anything. I went back in to the apartment. My husband wasn't there, so I waited. When he came in, I said right away, "Let's go to the doctor." Sam didn't ask why or what; within a moment he was ready to leave.

The doctor asked me when my last period was. I didn't know anything about a period; no one had ever explained it to me. I had experienced it only once during the time I spent in hiding, and that was it. Between the hunger and the fear that defined our way of life during the war, my period never came. I replied, "I don't know." I believe the doctor understood who I was, that I was young and had not led a normal life. He nodded to himself.

When he asked me to remove my clothes, I refused. I knew that all he wanted was to perform a standard checkup, yet I wouldn't allow it. No one was allowed to touch me but Sam. I said, "You'll have to call in my husband." My insistence that no man but my husband touch me, not even a doctor, remained throughout my entire life. I was one of a kind, and sometimes people even made fun of me for it, but I didn't care.

The doctor called Sam in, and spoke to me as to a child. He explained to me that I would soon feel something kicking me.

"When you feel that, you should come in right away." Two weeks later, I felt it.

Quietly, to myself, I wished I had my mother by my side, and I cried. It was just the time a girl needs her mother's presence, knowledge and support. I didn't know what to do. Yet nature takes its course, whether we are ready or not. I gave birth on August 8, 1946 in the Förenwald DP camp. My son Steve was born weighing only five pounds. He was too small to be circumcised at eight days old. But he was alive, and slowly he got bigger and stronger, until it was hard to make the connection between that small, frail baby and the strong man he grew up to be.

Life in Förenwald

For an interim camp, life in Förenwald was good. We were surrounded by thousands of refugees like ourselves, so we could at least be certain that we would not be persecuted or endangered as we had been in Chelm. Everyone in the DP camp had a dream of going somewhere, and this way of living for the future made people more agreeable about their present circumstances. I rarely talked to anybody. I was not afraid of my neighbors in the camp, but that did not mean I trusted them. Baby Steve was with me all the time and I spoke to him in Yiddish.

Our camp was a center of an orthodox religious community. As camp inhabitants, we had very little contact with the outside, but there was a rich educational and cultural life that developed within its borders. There was a school for children, an ORT vocational training institute, and a yeshiva (religious academy) with 150 students. The yeshiva in Förenwald also served as the administrative headquarters for all the yeshivot in the American zone. The camp also supported theatrical and musical activity and published a weekly newspaper entitled *Bamidbar* [the Hebrew name for the Book of Numbers, lit. "in the desert"], which became a medium of literary expression for the camp inhabitants.

There was a central kitchen where food was cooked in

mass quantities. We could go there and stand in line for the food, which wasn't my style. Instead, my husband Sam provided for us by getting chickens and taking them to the shochet. This time no chicken flew away. I had a kitchen, and I would prepare meals based on cooked chicken. We lived in a large room, with two large cupboards in the middle. On the other side lived a woman with two children. That's the way the camp had divided the apartment.

I don't know how I did it. I don't know how I knew to bake and cook. I had no idea how to raise a baby, but I was lucky enough to have a neighbor girl there who answered my questions and taught me what to do. I had only thirteen diapers for Steve, and I would wash them, boil them, dry them and press them every day.

When Sam was home, we spent all of our free time together. The camp was not closed off, and we'd go out on nice walks on Saturdays, as a family. The trees in that area were particularly beautiful. One time a film was even screened in the camp, and we saw it along with everyone else.

Life was dynamic in the camp. It was common to see people moving in and out. The woman who shared our apartment with her two children left shortly after Steve was born, perhaps for a better arrangement within the camp or off to a more permanent settlement. A single Hungarian man took her place. He was a very active man; unlike the single mother, he took advantage of our kitchen and used to bake and cook with fervor. His other hobbies included illegal peddling, for which he was arrested. I didn't know exactly what his offense was, as I was too naïve to ask questions.

When he was taken off to jail, he left all his belongings, including whatever money or gold he had, in my possession. He trusted me with everything but the clothes he had on his body when he left. I don't remember how long he was away, but when he came back he found everything just the way it had been when he'd last seen it. I hadn't moved a thing. He looked at me and said, "I've never seen anybody so honest. You didn't even look inside to see what I had." His surprise and awe brought me great pride.

America knocks on our door

Just like everybody else in the camp, we were registered to leave
Germany for a better life. We had registered to go to Palestine or to
America, whichever opened up first. Finally, there was room for us
on board a ship heading for the shores of Palestine. A big container
was packed with all of our belongings. I had an electric oven, and
it was in there. We didn't want to carry furniture, but we took
clothes and pots and pans, everything we needed. We were ready to
leave.

Yossel had decided that he would go where all the other
orphans seemed to be headed – to Palestine. However, as was
often the case with ships carrying illegal Jewish immigrants to
Palestine, his ship was diverted, and he ended up in Cyprus. My
brother Menachem was meant to come and join me in the DP
camp, but was instead taken to Italy, where he boarded a ship for
Palestine that met with the same obstacle. In Cyprus, both of my
brothers met. I received a letter from Yossel, in which he begged
me to come. Yossel missed me dearly. I had already been pregnant
when he left, and he had put his hand on my stomach and spoken
a blessing.

My reunion with my brothers seemed at hand; they would
eventually make the short distance from Cyprus to Palestine, and
my new family was headed there as well. Sam went to the Förenwald
offices in order to give up his DP camp registration passport, at
which point he was supposed to be given a number and information
about when and how we were going to leave for Palestine. Meanwhile,
men had arrived at our apartment to pick up our packed luggage,
but they declined to take anything that was marked with my name.
At the offices, Sam was told: "We're sorry, sir. You have a baby, and
this transport is already overloaded. You can't get on it with a baby
that young. Why don't you wait, and you can go over with the next
transport."

I could not hide my disappointment when Sam broke the
news to me. He explained what he'd been told, and I blurted out,
"Oy vey!" It was time for us to leave. I wanted desperately to leave

already, I couldn't stand it. Sam said, "I'm sorry. I couldn't argue with them. We'll just have to wait and get on the next transport."

Then we heard a knock on the door. American officials stood at our doorstep and let us know that we were being called to go to the USA. They had issued a visa for us. Others might have seen this as good news, even a miracle, but I was overwhelmed with confusion. I had two brothers in Cyprus, near Palestine. I didn't know what to do. I wanted to leave, but I could not decide which way to go.

Good advice

My mother and father were gone. Sam was as young as I was. I needed advice. We had a fateful decision ahead of us. There were a handful of people from my hometown who lived near me in the DP camp, and I turned to one of these men for advice. He was older than I, and so I counted on his wisdom. I told him the situation in the simplest way and ended with the truth, "I don't know what to do."

He thought for a second and said, "You know what, Rochaleh, you should go to Israel."

It occurred to me to ask him, "Where are you planning to go?"

He answered, "Oh, well, *we're* going to America."

His answer made me uneasy. I knew that the minute we'd arrive in Palestine, they'd take Sam into the army. Nevertheless, that was where I wanted to be, in the Land of the Jews, along with my two brothers. This man's conflicting advice had only served to deepen my confusion. I said to Sam, "Come on, let's go to Wolfe."

Wolfe was a kind man. During my pregnancy, he had helped arrange for the doctor to see me. We went in to him for advice. He thought about it and said, "Rochaleh, go to America. From America, if you don't like it, you can go to Israel any time. Go, be successful and help your poor brothers."

I liked the way he put it. I wrote a letter to Cyprus, to my brothers, and I told them I had decided to go to America.

Farewell to Förenwald

We had stayed in Germany from 1944 to 1949. For years we were registered with the American Consulate, but no country was willing to take us in. At the time, I was very angry about our situation. I often thought, 'How is it possible that no one wants us?' The biggest and most powerful countries in the world turned us away, claiming we were a liability. I knew deep in my heart how wrong they were. We were an asset. President Roosevelt could have taken in so many more Jews, people that would have accomplished great things and added so much to American culture. The Jewish immigrants were not ones to go on welfare; they worked hard and contributed to society. However, the world had been taught to hate us, and sadly it seemed that even amongst the allies, our liberators, many had learned that hatred.

The Displaced Persons Act of 1948, though still largely restrictive toward the Jews, was our salvation. In accordance with it, we were able to obtain visas. Each city in the USA was allotted a certain number of refugees they were able to accept. Most of my friends from the DP camp were already in New York, Los Angeles or Chicago, or they were headed there. I was being sent to Cincinnati, Ohio. I had never heard of that place, and had no idea where it was.

I stood in the American Consulate's office and begged them to send me and my family to a city I had actually heard of. "I don't know where Cincinnati is," I repeated. "I've never heard of it!" They told me that if I didn't want the visa, I could give it back. For them it was just a job, they dealt with visas and quotas and numbers, but for me, it was my entire future on the line!

Passing up on the visa and staying in Germany was not an option. I sat and cried about having to go to Cincinnati when some Jews who had happened to overhear my pleas approached me. They told me they had been to Cincinnati, that it was a good place and that there were Jews living there as well. Their words and their kindness soothed my concerns. I knew then that my family and I were heading for Cincinnati, and I hoped the city would be good to us.

The transport was supposed to leave on Passover, which was

something Rachel would not do. So our departure was delayed. In the meanwhile we stayed in another camp and visited the consulate, where we were interviewed several more times. Then we left for America from Hamburg.

On the boat

The boat ride to America was a difficult experience. I was sick for the entire trip. My baby boy Steve was begging for food, crying that he was hungry. When we left Germany, Steve was two years and eight months old, and he had never before uttered that word, *hungry*, not the way he did on the boat. I had hoped to go through the rest of my life without hearing any of my children ever cry that word. His tears broke my heart, but the minute I stepped out of our cabin and smelled food a wave of weakness washed over me, and I thought I was dying. It was not a pleasant boat ride, and I was deeply relieved when it was over.

When we arrived, I was the last one to leave the deck because my son had fallen down and hurt himself. The people on the boat took care of him, with my help. I knew what to do by then. I was no longer new to motherhood. But I was new to America. I didn't know a word in English, and neither did Sam. I didn't know anybody in America, but my husband did. He knew people from Turzysk who had arrived in America before us. He also had family here as well – an old distant relative of his, whom we referred to as a "second-hand grandpa," lived in Boston. He and his family were wonderful people. In Cincinnati itself Sam had a distant aunt. It was a source of comfort to us that we were not heading toward a strange new world, completely alone.

Not even seven dollars

Sam's "grandpa" from Boston had sent us five dollars, and his aunt added two more. These seven dollars were all we had in our pocket when we entered America. However, when the officials at customs saw that we were carrying American money, they promptly took it away. "You'll get it when you leave the country," they said, as if hoping we had not come to stay.

Some people from Turzysk picked us up. It was a welcome rush of relief, not to be alone during those first moments in a country where everything seemed bigger than what Sam and I had ever known. They took us to lunch at a nice restaurant. I was in another world altogether, and at first I didn't like it. A woman who was a distant cousin of Sam's was there, and the dress she wore was open and revealing. Such a sight was completely new for me. I had never seen people dressed like that in Germany, nor in my childhood in Poland.

However, the overall first impression was a good one, due to the kindness of Sam's friends. Those Turzysk Jews were absolutely wonderful. The minute they met me, they fell in love with me. One of the men, seeing that we were children who had had a child of their own, said to us, "Children, go to Cincinnati, but if you don't like it, here's my telephone number." Not long after that, we were on the move again.

Cincinnati

The name "Cincinnati" loomed over us. It was our life's great unknown. Little did we know that far from being an unknown city, Cincinnati occupied a prominent place in the history of the development of Jewish secular and religious life in the United States. Cincinnati was not only the oldest Jewish community west of the Allegheny Mountains, it had also been an institutional center of American Reform Judaism for a century by the time we arrived. *The American Israelite*, the longest-running Jewish weekly still published in the country to this day, opened for business in the city in 1854.

It had also been home to German Jews for over a century. During the 1830s, quite a number of German Jews had arrived in the city. On September 19, 1841, the B'nei Yeshurun Congregation was organized by the Germans, and was incorporated under the laws of the state on February 28, 1842. In 1866, the congregation built the architecturally notable Plum Street Temple, now known as the Isaac M. Wise Temple.

Plum Street is notable for having been the first of a number of American Moorish Revival synagogues. Many American congregations built Moorish Revival synagogues with façades inspired by Plum Street. All examples of similar architecture in Germany were destroyed by Hitler. Plum Street is among the oldest synagogue buildings still standing in the United States. As a daily paper wrote at the time, "Cincinnati had never before seen so much grandeur pressed into so small a space." I, too, was impressed by its beauty: its three-part, twin-domed façade. Its minarets, rose window and basilica-style arch filled me with a sense of Jewish pride.

Of course, the Jews only made up a small percentage of Cincinnati, roughly five percent at their peak, and even then our shared heritage did not assure that they would accept us as family. But it was of great comfort to know that there was a Jewish community we could join. Cincinnati was an exciting place to be during those postwar years, as the city unveiled a master plan for urban renewal that would result in a modernization of the inner city. Rachel and I were going to experience the city's evolution firsthand, as it became the backdrop for our own evolution. The beginning, however, was rough, as the city did not exactly welcome us with open arms...

The toilet room

I hadn't the slightest idea what Cincinnati was going to be like. The paperwork had been arranged by Sam's aunt, with the help of a Gentile friend. They had also arranged a room for us in Cincinnati. We were looking forward to meeting them; so far our experience with those who wished to help us had been warm and encouraging. This time, however, we were in for a disappointment.

Just as my uncle in Chelm had disliked Sam for no reason at

all, it was quickly apparent that Sam's aunt disliked me. As a direct result she disliked Sam as well, for having chosen me as his wife and bringing me into their world. It was an instantaneous dislike that was obvious from the moment his aunt and cousin came to pick us up at the train station and drive us to their home. She gave me headaches right away.

When Sam asked for water for our son Steve, she refused to let him open the refrigerator door. "Water costs money!" she cried. The insult deepened when she took us to our room. We had been told that she had prepared a room for our small family to stay in, but in fact she had chosen to put us up in her spare toilet room. She had taken the toilet itself out and replaced it with a bed, but the room itself was unmistakable. All she had set out for us was this one bed, which we were to share. In the privacy of our toilet bedroom, Sam said to me, "What is this? At least in the DP camp we had water and our own apartment!"

Her behavior toward us was more hurtful than the living conditions she afforded us. When my little boy Steve wanted something, she told him that he was no good. He was such a beautiful, nice child that it hurt me to hear her speak to him like that. She took all of our clothes, including a suit, and threw them into a washing machine. It was not kindness that made her rush to wash our clothes; rather it was her belief that, "dirty refugees" that we were, we'd come into her home with flies and other bugs and dirt on our bodies. There are no words for how demeaning it was.

She introduced us to another family, related to Sam by virtue of being related to her. Luckily for us, they were wonderful people. They lived far away, and they drove in to pick us up to spend the day with us. "Don't worry," they said to us. We hadn't said a thing about our concerns, but they understood how we must be feeling, living with that aunt. "This is a good country," they assured us.

When we came home, the doors were locked. We couldn't even get in to our small toilet room. Finally someone opened the door, but not before we had to contemplate spending the night on the street.

An American worker

During our first days in America, life moved fast. Before I knew it, my name had been changed; Bojmel became Boymel and Shulem was changed to Sam by the immigration office. One moment we were in a restaurant in New York with people from Turzysk, old friends as well as people with whom we shared a bond, and the next moment we were living in a toilet in Cincinnati. We arrived there on a Thursday, and on the following Sunday I already had my first American job.

They were constructing a Jewish school in Cincinnati, the Hafetz Haim building. Rachel said, "You should go over there and ask for a job." I agreed and headed over to the site. I introduced myself and said, "Could you give me some honest work? Even for a few days?" I was a young man with a family, and I believe this was a deciding factor. They replied, "We can give you a job for three days."

Rabbi Eliezer Silver was the head of the newly founded school and a very famous rabbi. He was the one who had said, "Give him the job." Rabbi Silver paid me $30 for the three days of work, and I believe the money came from his own pocket. He felt sorry for me.

We had met before in the DP camp. Rabbi Silver had visited Förenwald in order to bring Jews to America to be rabbis and *shochets*, to enrich the religious Jewish life in Cincinnati. I was in line when he was picking men for these jobs. There wasn't a man there who didn't want to be picked by Rabbi Silver and return with him to America.

He asked me, "Are you a *shochet*?"

"No," I said.

He asked, "Are you a *mohel* [ritual circumciser]?"

"No," I said.

That was it for our encounter in Förenwald. He couldn't take me as a *shochet* or a *mohel*, but when our paths crossed again in Cincinnati he could take me as a construction worker. He smiled at me and said, "I remember you. You were with a jeep, dressed like an officer."

"That was me," I replied. "I've made it to America."

A slave worker

Shortly after the construction job ended, a Jewish woman by the name of Rachael was sent on behalf of the synagogue to take me around and help me get a job. Such pairings were commonly arranged at the time as a means of helping Jewish immigrants overcome language barriers and culture shock in their search for employment. Women would volunteer to accompany refugees on the job hunt, direct them to the right opportunities and, if needed, translate and speak English for them.

This help was crucial because people looked down on refugees, and we were faced with many ugly stereotypes. A common one was that we stank, that we didn't wash. Unfortunately, the women who were sent to help refugees often held the same degrading opinions about them. This lady said to me, "Look, when they ask you questions, don't say anything. Let me do all the talking, and we'll be all right."

She took me straight to a furniture dealership downtown. It was run by three brothers who greeted us at the storefront. All three were dressed very nicely. She told the eldest, in English, that many refugees had recently arrived, and that they were in need of jobs. As one of the brothers looked me over, she went up to him and gave him a kiss. She stepped aside to kiss another brother, then the last one as well.

At that point I figured that the job was as good as mine. An African-American man was standing in the corner. The first brother looked the both of us over and stated that he paid the African-American $25 each week, and that he was willing to pay me $18 each week if I wanted his job.

They asked that I carry a refrigerator from the cellar to the third floor. There was no elevator. They slung a big rope around my neck and I crawled up the steps, the weight of the refrigerator bearing down on my shoulders, dragging behind me and threatening to pull me back down every step I had gained. I was young and strong and able to do it, but it was grueling work. When I had made it to the top, the man said to me, "You're all right." I was new to the language, and I didn't know what he had meant by that. After that they had me take a big stove up the same way. While I crawled up with it, the lady gave him another kiss.

When I came back out, she seemed very proud of herself. She said, "You see, he let go of the African-American who worked for him for so many years, and he gave you this job for $18. My grandfather, when he came in the 1800s, only got $3."

The boss said to me, "You haven't said anything. Do you want the job?"

I had done what he asked me to do without saying a word, while I considered my options. I turned to this Rachael and asked, "How much would I need for renting a room?"

She said, "Well, a room will cost you $45."

I knew that the room that she spoke of was the kind that did not even have a washing room in it; we'd have to go out in the hallway and share a communal bathroom with other tenants, and I knew my wife would not want to do that.

I asked, "And how much will I need for food? I don't want anything else, you see, just to pay for the rent and the food. How will I manage that with only $18?"

Rachael was upset. "My grandfather worked for $3 and you won't work for $18?" She sneered at me as if I disgusted her. I didn't mind her; I wasn't there to please her or to measure up to her grandfather. I had one objective in mind – to support my family. She dropped me off and left in a huff. One condescending woman or another did not bother me. I had survived Hitler and Stalin. I knew I was going to be all right.

The streets of Cincinnati

The next day I headed out on my own. No help at all was better than the kind of help offered me the previous day. I walked toward the electric buses, without a clear destination in mind. All I knew was that I was young, able-bodied and willing to work. I believe that my predicament and my attitude toward it were visible in my eyes.

A woman passing by stopped and asked me where I was headed. "Downtown," I replied, assuming that I would find the biggest concentration of businesses there. "But I have no money," I admitted. She gave me thirteen cents, and I thanked her.

I got on the first bus I saw. The bus conductor was a Christian German who had probably been working there for years, and he spoke to me in German. I spoke honestly to everybody that day, and so I said to him, "Look, I need a job." He nodded and said, "I'll take you downtown to 6th and Vine." Thanks to this bus conductor I learned that this was the Jewish area; there were Jewish stores of all kinds up and down the block. I tried to give him my thirteen cents, and he immediately said, "Put it in your pocket." He wouldn't take my money. He said he'd heard stories about what we'd gone through in the concentration camps. I was surprised – the majority of people we met seemed to have no knowledge of our experience or sympathy for us as survivors.

I thanked the man warmly and got off the bus at the stop he'd recommended. The names on the signs and awnings told me I'd arrived at the right place. Some of the stores were kosher, and I decided to walk into them. The first was a kosher *shochet* who slaughtered chickens. He was from Jerusalem, and so I was able to speak to him in Yiddish. I asked if I could get a job picking feathers. He said, "Go talk to the boss, Schreiber."

Schreiber was sitting in another room. I knocked on his door, and he called me in. He spoke Yiddish as well. His eyes were cold. He barely looked me over before he said, "We have no need for more people. I have a couple of African-Americans, and they work for cheap. You're a refugee, I can't give you work." The way he said "refugee" was as if it was a dirty word. I walked out.

The next store was a vegetable stand. I approached a Jewish family. The older family members could speak Yiddish. The mother of the family handed me a rotten apple to eat. I looked around and saw that there were plenty of ripe fruits and vegetable there; it was a big store. I was in an unfortunate situation, and handouts were welcome, but this was more of an insult. Still, I could not show my emotions, not until I was turned down. This happened quickly enough. "We have African-American workers, and they work for cheap," they told me. "We're sorry, but we can't give you a job."

My wife was waiting at home with a small child. What could I do? I had nothing in my pocket, let alone savings in a bank somewhere. Every rejection was like a blow, but I had no choice. I could not return home empty-handed. The thought of returning to my wife Rachel and my son Steve with nothing to show for my day hurt more than anything else. I pressed on.

"Fleischer's" Kosher Salami*

I walked around for quite a while before passing by a sign that read "Fleischer" — Kosher Salami." I had arrived around lunchtime, just in time to see ten or fifteen non-Jewish Germans walk into the shop, order salami and gobble it down with a beer outside. I approached the men, who were happy to hear another man speak their language. They exclaimed, "Oh, a German!"

I said, "Yes, but I am Jewish."

"You're lucky! You're in the right place! The boss here is Jewish," one of the men told me.

This German was a good man, and he could tell that I was hungry. I had been running around downtown all day with nothing but a rotten apple in my stomach. He took out hot dogs and handed them to me with a piece of bread. Once my hunger had abated, this man took me in to see the boss. He was very kind in his introduction of me. "Max," he said to the owner, "I brought you in a nice guy, a refugee who comes from Poland. He's good and he lost everybody, and he needs a job."

Max Fleischer eyed me with interest. His business was doing very well; Fleischer was shipping meat all over the country. "You've been in the concentration camps?" he asked me. "Where are you from?"

---

*   A pseudonym.

I told him in short where I'd come from, what I'd seen and what I'd been through.

"Well, my father comes from Vilna," he said. "He and Manischewitz came to Cincinnati. My father opened the salami and corned beef and cold cuts place, and now we're doing well." He had not asked any further questions, and so I remained silent, waiting for a word from him. Finally, as if concluding out loud a deliberation conducted in his mind, he said, "Yes, I can give you a job."

He pushed a button, and Joe Bloom came over. He was the foreman. Joe Bloom and Max Fleischer spoke in English, and Max told him I was a refugee in need of a job. I was then told, in German, "I've got a job for you. Come down to the basement."

The job was in the freezer. My duties were to cut and pickle the meat. In order to make corned beef, I had to learn how to inject spices into the meat. The meat needed to be washed to make it kosher; it soaked for half an hour in salt and for an additional hour in water. This had to be at a very cold temperature. Because the job required me to stand in the cold the whole time and work with uncooked meat, he gave me plastic to put over my clothes. "The pay," he told me, "is $25 a week."

This was just fine by me. It was news I could come home with proudly.

The landlady's hungry children

Sam's distant relatives, whom we had visited once before, were kind enough to introduce us to a woman who was divorced with three children. They knew that we were desperate to move out of the toilet room, and that she, having lost her husband, would welcome the extra income from renting out a room.

We were relieved to move out of the toilet room and into a real room. In this new room we even had a crib for Steve, which made me very happy. I had felt that he was too young to sleep in a bed, but in the confined toilet room we'd had no choice. Every night I'd been afraid that Sam or I would hurt him accidentally during the night, in our sleep.

Our rent for this room was $40, including free use of the kitchen. It was expensive for just the room, but prices were high at the time as a result of the war with Korea. Soldiers were coming home in large numbers and were met with a shortage of work and real estate.

My husband Sam was already making money at this point from his job at the Fleischer butcher shop, and his aunt wanted to take money from him for the time we had spent at her place. She was just cold-hearted enough to demand payment for helping out a family member in need. It was her husband who stopped her. "No," he said. "Sam has a wife and a child. Don't do this to his wife."

Our new landlady would come home from work, prepare food for her children and head off to see her boyfriend. A few hours later, her children were hungry again, but she was gone. This situation was a real hardship for me, because whatever I put in the refrigerator, her children ate before I could get to it. I didn't have the heart to reprimand them because I had been a hungry child myself at one point. I couldn't talk to them in English. I said, "Come," and gestured to them. They followed me into the kitchen. I opened up the refrigerator and pointed at each and every one of my items. I said in Yiddish, "This is mine. This – is mine. This – is mine. Do you understand?" They understood, but they were children, they were hungry and there was no stopping them eating out of their own refrigerator.

"You think you had it bad"

I set out for the Fleischer butcher shop every day at 4 a.m. before the break of dawn. Our new home was far from my workplace so I had to take two buses to get there on time. My workday started before sunrise and ended after sunset. When I returned home, my hands were frozen and aching from tending to the icy meat for hours on end. My wife would then pour hot water over my hands, reviving them so that I could move my fingers again.

I worked in the freezer for five years. No matter the season outdoors, my life was one long winter. All the while, we could not shake off the feeling that we were different, that we were "refugees," but we did our best to disregard this. All we could do was work hard. On Saturdays we prayed at the same synagogue as the Fleischer family, who were very religious people. At the synagogue they treated us like refugees, either ignoring us or showing pity. At work, Fleischer would sometimes give me bones to take home. I thanked him and took them to my wife Rachel, who used them to make soup. She fed the landlady's children as well as our Steve. I was polite and a good worker; I earned raises and saw my salary go up to 40 dollars a week. But most importantly, I was slowly learning the business.

Because we needed every cent we could make, Rachel often spent her evenings babysitting. A circle of Jewish women would bring their babies over to the apartment of one of them, and Rachel would show up to babysit up to ten babies at a time. They paid her a mere twenty-five cents for the whole evening. These women were rich, yet they wouldn't offer my wife any more money for being much more than a babysitter; ten children required a kindergarten teacher. Rachel was desperate for work, and so she agreed.

One night I arrived to pick Rachel up from the apartment where she'd been babysitting. When she opened the door, I saw her face covered with blood. One of the children had climbed onto the refrigerator, and as she attempted to take him down, the child had taken a bottle and thrown it in her face. The kid was laughing as he did it, Rachel told me. He was as spoiled as his parents were.

I confronted the child's mother. I said to her, "We don't need your quarter. Look at what your child did to my wife. She's a human being. She went through things you're lucky you never saw."

They didn't care. One of these women actually said to my wife, "You think you had it bad in Germany, in the camps? We had it much worse here. My daughter couldn't get a date. The American soldiers went away, and there were no suitors left for her."

Rachel never returned to work as a babysitter. She found a different job, this time as a caretaker for older women. She watched over them, helped them and cleaned for them. We learned to keep quiet about the horrors we had lived through. It was clear that for these people it was nothing. The pain of mentioning it to a disrespectful audience was too much. My mother's wish that I share my story was set aside for the time being.

Free furniture – for a price

It wasn't long before our hard work allowed us to move out of our rented room and into a place of our own. Sam worked long days, and so it was up to me to go out and find an apartment for our family. The market was a difficult one at the time, and I spoke no more than a few words in English, but after a long search I found an agreeable third-floor apartment.

We moved out on a Friday. I took Steve's crib along with our few possessions and stuffed them in a cab, and we left our divorced landlady for good. Our new apartment was empty. It didn't even have a stove or a refrigerator, but I was happy. The place was our own, shared with no one, and it was clean and painted. Ever since I was a little child, cleanliness had been extremely important to me. As long as it was clean, I knew I could make a home out of it.

In the stairwell, an elderly lady came up to me and asked, "How are you going to live like that? You don't have a stove, you don't have a refrigerator, and you don't have any furniture."

I shrugged and said, "I don't know." I hadn't gotten around to thinking of that yet; I was still enjoying the move itself, free of that divorcee's apartment.

She said, "You know what, there is a man that supplies furniture for every refugee."

I was used to being spoken to in this way. We weren't people then; we were "refugees." I said nothing, and the little old lady interpreted this as a yes. My husband was at work at Fleischer's butcher shop. By the time he came home at night, the old lady had already called the man in question and described my situation to him. Once he'd been satisfied that my family and I truly were refugees, his men showed up at my door and brought me a bedroom set, a refrigerator and a stove.

My husband Sam came home and stopped short. "Rachel, what did you do?" he asked. When he'd left that morning, we had nothing. Now, all of a sudden, our place was fully furnished. He asked himself the same thing I would have asked myself: how had we paid for all this?

I said, "I didn't do anything. I don't know where it came from."

Sam went down to our neighbors on the first and second floor, to learn where the furniture had come from. He came across the elderly lady, who told him, "It's from Mr. Levinson. He has a furniture store, and he gives all the refugees furniture."

Lo and behold, the following week I received a little book courtesy of Mr. Levinson that said I had to pay every week, until I had repaid a sum of a couple thousand dollars. I wasn't a dummy. The furniture was obviously not new; it looked like it had been repossessed from people who hadn't paid on time. I understood that he had taken advantage of me. Had it been up to me, I never would have bought any of the furniture he'd sent as a supposed gift. I would have bought something I liked. Yet we paid off every dollar he demanded. We weren't about to be indebted to a furniture store owner and con man. People often told us, "I wouldn't have paid." Perhaps they wouldn't have, but we did.

And so we had our first apartment. In the summer we were dying of heat, and in the winter we were freezing. The heating was shared by all three apartments in the building, but the neighbor below us used to shut it off before it could reach our floor so that she could have more heat at our expense. My little boy kept reopening it, which produced a grating sound of metal against metal, at which point they would climb up to our floor complaining that my Steve was being noisy. One time they rapped their fists so violently against our door that I thought I was back in the ghetto, and I started screaming. It was hell.

We lived a modest life. Between rent, basic necessities and paying for the furniture, we all but used up our income. At least that was what Sam believed. I made a point of putting away $10 a week from whatever Sam brought me, no matter how much it was, for a rainy day. I knew that if something happened to us, we didn't have anybody and we didn't have anything. I didn't tell Sam about the $10. If we were to need money some day, for whatever reason, we would have some. In the meanwhile we made do with ten dollars short, and sometimes even less, since I had somebody else to support: my brother in Israel.

Yossel

My two remaining brothers arrived in Israel together aboard the *Exodus*. Our family had two cousins over there, and they took them in at first. Yossel and Menachem were quick to join the Israeli Army, which was then fighting for its independence. This war cost Yossel his life. He was one of the 6,000 men and women who fell in the creation of the Jewish state. My brother Menachem lived through the war and emerged without a family. Israel was a fledgling state, existing in poverty. Menachem couldn't make a living, and so every month my brother got a package from me. He was the only sibling I had left; I only wished I could have been of greater help to him.

News of Yossel's death arrived in the form of a telegram. Before the telegram reached me, I saw it in a dream. In the dream, I was reunited with my brother Menachem, but it was not a happy reunion. His face was grief-stricken, and he told me, "We lost our brother Yossel." I woke up in tears and said to Sam, "Something is wrong." The telegram had already come, but Sam had hidden it from me. He was waiting for the right time to break the news. When I finally laid eyes on the telegram, it said exactly what my brother Menachem had told me in the dream: "We lost our brother Yossel, and now it's me and you."

I was screaming; not crying but hollering in tears. I had

survived the Holocaust with him, only to lose him now? It was crazy, and it drove me crazy. Two officers showed up at our doorstep after one of the neighbors called the police. They had thought that my husband was beating me, as if such a thing was possible. When the policemen arrived, we were unable to explain ourselves. I was beside myself with shock, and Sam didn't have enough English in him. He simply handed the telegram over to the police officer, who read it and understood.

The policeman went over to the synagogue and informed the rabbi of what he had seen. The rabbi came over to talk to me and counsel me, but I would not listen to a word he said. My mind raced in a circle, asking only, "Why? Why did it happen?" My question was directed at God, and I knew that I wouldn't get an answer.

Why?

I shut down. A nervous breakdown plunged me into depression. I stopped taking care of my baby, and I no longer talked to my husband. My mind was in Israel, where my baby brother had been killed, where my sole surviving brother had to live with this loss all alone. Everything that took place in America was a million miles away from me, too hazy to focus on, too muffled to hear.

I was taken to the hospital, but I was not a real participant in what happened to me there. I cannot say how long I remained hospitalized, hours or days. When I returned to our apartment, a nurse from the hospital would come and visit me every single day. She did her best to talk to me. Then she sent a social worker to talk to me. I was predisposed to dislike any American social worker; no American could truly understand what I'd been through. But when she talked to me about my child and my husband, she said, "You have to take care of them." I knew she was right.

She took care of Steve in the meantime. Sam helped as best he could, but his work kept him away from the house during most hours of the day. The social worker decided that my best chance of recovery was to go away with the child, change my environment and recuperate in a different setting. She kept saying that I was intelligent enough, that I would know how to do it myself, without anybody's help.

All I kept saying at the time was, "Why, why, why, why, why?" It was my mantra of grief. Looking back on it, I wonder, just how much of that can a family take? Mine never said a word. They never asked me to stop talking. However, my little boy Steve was crying with me. It hurt him to see his mother like that, and his tears made me realize it was wrong.

Healing

My husband had a cousin in New York City by the name of Rebecca. They called her and described my situation. Rebecca said, "By all means, send her over." Sam stayed at home in Cincinnati while the baby and I went to New York. I'm sure he was lonely, working long hours and returning to an empty apartment, but he knew it was for the best. He knew his wife needed to get better.

New York City was home to many Jews, both before and after the war. A few of them were from my hometown or Sam's. When I arrived there, the first thing Rebecca did was to take me to meet people from my husband's town, Turzysk. Several of them were the ones who had taken us out to a restaurant on our first day in America, and they were just as nice to me now.

However, this visit was of a different nature altogether. Rebecca had the time to show me more of their way of life. One family from Turzysk had bought a kiosk. The wife of this family took me around to see many people, from Turzysk and other places. She took me to see their poor homes. They lived in big, brown and grey housing projects. Each apartment was overcrowded, and each bed was meant for at least two people, if not four. I listened to their stories, I looked into their homes, and I wanted to throw up. It was awful.

I let the sights seep in to me in silence. I thought to myself,

'Now that I'll never do. I'm not going to put my baby in a bed with so many people.' This went on for two weeks. Rebecca wouldn't let me go home; she saw that I was getting a little better, and she wanted to keep exposing me to shades of life that kept me grounded. When New York had begun to exhaust its potential, I spent a few days in Boston with my husband's "grandfather." He and his family were the nicest people, and staying with them seemed like a natural continuation of the healing process.

On one of my walks in New York City with Steve and Rebecca, I was suddenly grabbed from behind, hugged and kissed. The man who had done this was named Isaac, and he was from my hometown of Ozierany. He had been a good friend of my brother Meyer, so he was a few years older than me. His happiness at running in to me in the street was powerful. Through him I found more people from my hometown and received many invitations, which comforted me.

I began to feel more stabilized, but I knew I was not well yet. An older man from Ozierany whom I had met through Isaac invited me over often; he was eager to talk to someone, anyone, about a town lost forever. When he had me as an audience, he told me about my family, about my mother, about my grandfather. He was close to my mother's age and as a teenager had been very much in love with her. He remembered his disappointment when she'd gotten married to a man from Warsaw, my father.

This man's wife became so jealous that I was forced to ask him to stop talking to me. Sam's grandfather had also begun to fear that I would run off with someone else, and that his grandson Sam would be all alone. I sensed this, and his grandmother told me so outright. I said, "It has never crossed my mind." I had my own reason for minimizing contact with this man from my hometown: all his talk of the past brought tears to my eyes, and I hadn't come to New York to cry. I couldn't take it. It hurt me so much, the way he talked about how beautiful my mother was, the way he described her long black hair and beautiful features.

I had been away for a month now, and it was too long. I wanted to go home. That was the final sign I needed in order to feel assured that I was better. When I came home, I learned that people who hadn't seen me for a month had assumed I'd left my husband. The craziest things came to people's minds. I sat with Sam for hours and described everything I'd seen in New York and how it had given me renewed appreciation for all that we had. I had a family. I had a fresh little apartment. I had big bills to pay, but it was all right. Sam believed every word I said, and he felt the same way. Our family was back on track.

The boarder

After returning to Cincinnati, I walked away from babysitting altogether. I simply couldn't do it anymore; it was emotionally taxing and the pay was humiliating. Instead, I took in a boarder. This meant giving up my dining room, but it enabled me to send more money to Menachem and to more easily put aside my rainy-day money. The room was rented out to a young Jewish man for $20 a week. In return, I gave him clean clothes and food.

After the first week I made the worst discovery: he was a dirty man. God forgive me, I would take the sheets off his bed using two fingertips. The sheets were stained in the shape of a man – he was that dirty. He didn't clean the bathtub after he used it, either. I didn't like it and wanted to throw him out, but couldn't, not on account of cleanliness, and more importantly, not without having a sure replacement on hand. My husband Sam understood how much this bothered me, and he helped me make our home livable, despite our filthy boarder, by regularly cleaning the bathtub after him.

I needed the money, so I put up with this unwanted roommate. I was helping my brother, sending him packages all the time. Later, another guy by the name of Jack came over to check out the room. After making sure that Jack was willing to replace my current boarder, I asked the filthy man to leave. Jack was immaculately clean. He was my kind of boarder.

Self-educated

Neither Sam nor I could afford to go to school and formally study English. I began to pick up the language simply by being around Americans, but that was not enough. I made it a habit to go to the library, collect a pile of books and bring them back to the apartment. I didn't read them for their stories; in fact it was a good while before I understood any of what I was reading at all. The apartment had a big window where I sat to read. When the sun set, I kept the light on until 2 a.m. I didn't use a dictionary. As long as I knew the ABCs, I could read.

I had a little radio on. I had no idea what the broadcasters were saying, and when songs came I had no idea what they were singing. I was always listening closely for the word "Israel," because I wanted to know what was going on over there. One day I got up in the morning, and the radio was playing. I'll never forget the moment when a certain song came on. It was "Charlie My Boy," and I realized that I could understand each and every word of it. I was a self-educated woman. I had taught myself to speak, read and write English.

At that time, Steve was attending kindergarten at the Jewish Center. He spoke English after a week in America, but spoke to Sam and me in Yiddish and in German, because we had been in Germany, and he'd had a babysitter there. When we first came to America, he would say "Mom, what are they saying? What kind of language are they using?" I explained it to him, and I bought books for him and I read them to him. When my kids grew up, I helped them with school. I was able to help them with their homework, read it to them and explain anything they might not understand. I know it's unbelievable, but that's my true story.

Patsy

In 1954, I became pregnant again and gave birth to our daughter Patsy, named after my mother, Pessa Fruma. We had to have an

English name for her, so we called her Patsy, but Patsy and Pessa were essentially the same name.

Pregnancies were never easy on me. I was sick for the whole nine months of my first pregnancy. After birth I required stitches. This was still in the DP camp, and I was very prone to infections there. My body tended to lose weight at first, rather than gain it. I was four months pregnant with Patsy before I found out. I lost twenty-two pounds and underwent two surgeries.

My head wouldn't stop aching. My doctors concluded that it was the result of an infection in my tonsils, and that they had to be removed. A very nice doctor, a Russian man, was the one who operated on me. I remember his kind smile, as he told me that I was a crybaby. The second surgery was also needed on account of an infection. The procedures were both successful. It helped that my doctor was so nice, and my family so supportive.

Patsy was born a healthy, beautiful baby girl. I was very happy to have a daughter and that Steve now had a little sister, but along with the joy it was also a very difficult time for me. I was a young woman with a very clear and narrow routine: I had to take care of my family, I had to help my brother, and I had to save some money. My life revolved around those goals. Sam would get up at 5 a.m. so I got up with him and fed him. Steve woke up and I took him to school. The rest of the day was spent taking care of the baby. I didn't complain, but I was happy to do what I had to do.

The car manufacturer

Sam had a hard time as well. He didn't like working for Fleischer. I didn't like two things: I didn't like that he had to work for somebody else, and I didn't like the fact that they had no feelings. We often discussed his options and his feelings about working at Fleischer. I said to my husband, "Sam, I want you to stay and work there and learn; learn how to cut meat. Maybe after you learn we'll go somehow and you'll open up your own butcher shop." After all, he was young and had arrived in America without a trade. Everybody had to have something they were able to do; this one was a plumber and that one was a carpenter, but we didn't have a trade.

Around that time we became friendly with another Jewish couple. Social events were rare for us, since we had no time for a social life, but managed to share a few dinners with this couple at our house. The husband kept badgering Sam about going to work for a car manufacturer. Sam reminded him, "They're not allowed to take people that aren't citizens. You know we aren't citizens yet." The man insisted that Sam should go and try to register there anyway. "It can't hurt," he reasoned.

And sure enough, the car factory accepted the both of them, even though neither was a citizen. They saw two young men, so they took them. Sam had to do very heavy work there, but they paid him $125 a week, a world of difference from the $40 he was making at Fleischer's. But unlike work in the freezer, Sam came home at night with heavy, despairing complaints. I was the type who saved a dollar, but I didn't want to do it on Sam's back. I wanted him to learn and advance, not to be a slave.

I said to Sam, "I don't want you to go there. Go back to Fleischer."

"You want me to leave $125 and go back to $40??" He asked.

I told him, "I don't want the $125. I don't want you to work on a line where you have to have someone replace you if you need to go to the bathroom. I want you to work somewhere where you can gain valuable knowledge."

The next morning he went back to the butcher. Fleischer raised his salary to $45. Life improved, and we managed to get by, but I was worried about the future, not the present. I knew that things were bound to change for us, but that we would have to make them change...

THE BUTCHER'S SHOP

Faye

Our youngest daughter, Faye, or Feygala as we called her in
Yiddish, was born on July 4, 1956. After the birth, the doctor
examined her, concluded that everything was fine and that I could
be discharged. We brought Faye home from the hospital, excited
to introduce her to her new home and her older brother and sister.
Not long after she settled in, I was changing her diaper when all of
a sudden an alarming shade of bright red caught my eyes. Faye was
bleeding. I rushed to the phone and called the doctor. By then I
spoke English, but the language nearly escaped me as I frantically
described what I saw to my doctor.

The doctor sent me to a specific drugstore. "Say your name
at the counter, and you'll get the right pills," he said. "Bring
them home and call me. I'll tell you what to do." What he hadn't
mentioned was their price: they came in packets of six pills for
$12. At the time, this was extremely costly, especially for people
of our modest means. Of course, there was no question that we
had to get them; Faye's health came first, above anything else.

I said to my husband, "Sam, I want you to go and ask for a
raise."

My husband said, "He's not going to give it to me."

I said, "Please, just go and ask for a raise."

We both knew that this was about more than Faye's pills. We had used the money I'd saved up to put a down payment on our own house, and now that one of our children had fallen ill, our balance was threatened. We had worked hard for years, and we deserved a basic level of financial security.

The scale

My son Steve used to come with me to the synagogue, where he'd see Max Fleischer sitting near the stage in his seat of honor. Steve was a little man; he understood everything that was going on and had his own opinion on the matter. That day he turned to me just before the service started and said, "I'm going to Fleischer to tell him that I have another sister and she's sick, and that he should give you a $5 raise."

I was proud of my son, but I wouldn't let him go. I said, "Steve'aleh, don't do it. He could fire me."

Sending my son to ask my boss for a raise at the synagogue was inappropriate, but I did share Steve's conviction: I had earned a raise, and I had an honest reason for demanding one. My son had wanted to do the asking for me, my wife also had urged me to ask, and now it was up to me. I woke up on Monday morning, stepped in to Max Fleischer's office, kissed his hand and his forehead and said, "Mr. Fleischer. I've never come to ask you for anything. But now I have another baby."

He huffed impatiently, "Well, why are you coming to tell me that?"

I said, "I have another baby girl, and she's so sick. I have to buy medication for her and pay doctors' bills."

Max Fleischer understood what I had come to ask for before I could spell it out. In response, he bent down to the garbage can that stood beside him on his office floor and pulled out a newspaper. He said, "You see, there are fifteen million people without a job, and you want a raise? Go away."

My eyes welled up. I walked out of the office and then out of the butcher shop, thinking to myself, "What will I tell my wife now?" I sat down on the concrete in front of the "Fleischer – Kosher Salami" sign and cried. Not only had I not gotten the raise we needed so badly, I had lost my job. I fixed my eyes on the pavement I had stepped on day in and day out for many years. At that moment it seemed foreign to me, as if I had suddenly become a stranger. I looked up and across the street and saw, displayed in the glass window of a shop, a scale for sale at $10. I knew that I had to have that scale. I got up, crossed the street and bought it. Without quite knowing it, I had made up my mind: I was going to open my own butcher's shop.

Papers from the rabbi

Sam came home with the unfortunate news. I was sad, though hardly taken by surprise. Fleischer had been a decent boss, better than others perhaps, but I had felt for a while now that he was taking advantage of Sam, as well as taking him for granted. I had very little opportunity to cry; it was dinner time, and the meal still had to be prepared even though we didn't know where the next one would be coming from.

Our whole family sat by the table that night. Sam and the kids ate while I fed the baby. After the children were full and the baby was put to sleep, I cleaned the kitchen and the house became nice and quiet. I sat back down at the kitchen table with Sam.

I said, "You know what you'll do? Tomorrow I want you to go to Rabbi Silver and ask him for the okay to open up a butcher's shop." You couldn't open a kosher butcher's shop without papers from the Rabbi.

Sam agreed. That very night he looked through ads in the paper and found a cash register he could buy for a very low price. The next day he met with Rabbi Silver, who was more than happy to provide him with the necessary papers. The Rabbi was pleased to be witnessing Sam's progression from a young officer in a DP camp, to a newcomer to America eager for work, and now, finally, to an entrepreneur.

Word got around to Fleischer that his former employee, Sam Boymel, was set on opening his own business. Fleischer quickly called Rabbi Silver. "If Boymel comes to you, don't give him the papers," he told him.

"He was already here, and I gave him his papers," Rabbi Silver replied. "What else do you expect him to do? The man came in and asked you for a raise. He has three kids!"

Fleischer hung up, furious. There was nothing he could do now.

The store

I had a scale, a register and papers from Rabbi Silver. It seemed that I was collecting all the necessary items for a shop that did not yet exist, but before I could feel that any of this was real, I needed to find the right space for my business. The process was quite similar to the first time I had arrived at 6th and Vine looking for a job, any job, with nothing in my pockets and barely a few words of English. I set to walking the streets, and instead of reading the signs, I looked up at them and imagined the words "Boymel – Kosher Meat" displayed upon them.

I came upon an empty store. It had been rented by a Jewish shopkeeper, now on his way out. The space had been emptied, and only a few movers were still around, packing the very last items. I asked them who the landlord was and learned that the owner of this recently vacated space was a German man, Mr. Shulty. They told me where I could find him.

His office was far away. Having no time or money to spare, I headed to him on foot. I walked for miles and miles, without any assurance that the place was even still for rent. Mr. Shulty let me in to his office. I told him, "I came to this country from Europe with nothing. Now I want to open a business."

He said, "What kind of business?"

I said, "A butcher's shop."

"No," Shulty shook his head. "That's no good. Butcher's shops smell, and there are people living upstairs."

I quickly said, "My shop will not smell. I won't be killing any cattle here. I'll be bringing in the meat frozen from somewhere, and everything in my shop will be clean."

Shulty looked into my eyes, and he believed me. "All right, I agree," he said. "But I will need three hundred dollars in advance. That'll be one month's rent and one month's deposit."

Of course I did not have such money on me, nor did I know where I could possibly get it, but at that moment I thanked him, shook his hand and promised to return with the money as soon as possible.

I came home and told my wife about my day. She listened, nodded, got up to go to the bedroom and returned holding $300 cash in her hand.

"Where did you get that money?" I asked, dumfounded.

"Don't worry," she said. "Go and rent the store."

Only later did I learn about my wife's habit of saving $10 at a time and hiding the money under our mattress. She would save every dollar that she could, and even when it added up to quite a bit of money she was not tempted to use it for anything but our future. When my son was just a little boy, he'd cry that he wanted a nickel for ice cream, but she wouldn't give it to him; the money was meant for bigger things, like a house for our family. And then, immediately after we bought our first house, she began saving again without hesitation, knowing that there were more big steps to be taken. Now the time had come once again to put Rachel's savings to use. I rented the store that very day.

The equipment

Other than the scale and the cash register, our new store stood empty. I needed equipment: freezers, refrigerated display counters and so on. I scoured the papers for deals. An article in the Cincinnati Enquirer reported that the IGA store had gone out of business. This was a big store that had been selling plenty of equipment. Now that they had gone under, their merchandise was on sale for very low prices. However, after having invested our mattress-savings in renting the store, we still could not afford most of the equipment.

I decided to turn to my fellow Jews for help. I went to Mr. Levinson, the same rich man who had sold us the free furniture that had put us in his debt for many months. I asked him for a $500 loan toward getting my butcher shop on its feet. Once my business was running, I promised he would get his money back. However, he wouldn't give it to me. He sent me to another man, who sent me to a third, promising, "If that guy signs, I'll sign." This third rich Jew barely heard me out before exclaiming, "I can't give you money! I have kids to put through college!" I was sorely disappointed. A lot of people had helped me over the years, but this time, not the Jews.

Though we didn't have the money, we also had nothing to lose. And so we made it a family outing: my wife, my son, my daughter, my youngest baby daughter and I all went out to the IGA store. We walked around, up and down the aisles. I was like a kid in a candy store – everything called out to me. I kept saying, "I could use this, and I could use this." The wheels and gears in my head were spinning. With all this equipment, our dream could become a reality.

An old Gentile man by the name of Mr. Mondor took notice of my little family, and the way my eyes glittered at all the equipment. Mondor walked over and introduced himself. He was retiring, and he had an only daughter. Since his son-in-law didn't want to work at his store, he was closing up.

He asked us, "Are you from Europe?"

"Yes," we told him.

He said, "And you have no money?"

My wife and I said in unison, "No."

"What about $50 a month?"

We admitted that yes, we could afford that.

"Well," he said, "Pick everything that you like. After you've picked it out, you can pay it back in installments of $50 a month, once you've settled in."

Excited, we did as he said. Soon we would have equipment,

and so we needed to be ready for its arrival. Steve, my wife and I all cleaned the store. Steve was very helpful. Once the store was clean, we faced a new challenge: we needed professionals to deliver and install the equipment. We needed movers, electricians, plumbers and so on. It would have been dangerous for us to attempt to do it all ourselves. Mr. Mondor smiled. He called the different professionals and said, "I want you to come and pick up all the equipment from the IGA store and bring it over to Boymel."

"Mr. Mondor," I said, "I don't have the money for this."

"Don't worry," he told me.

The equipment was brought in and set up in no time. Within a few days it was all there. We had a butcher shop. Now we needed meat.

The meat

I was well-acquainted with the packing house. When I still worked for Fleischer I used to go over there before dawn to pick up the meat. I knew, for instance, that when you bought meat you had to pay with cash, and I knew that I did not have that cash on hand. The packing house workers were Jews. They knew me well. They appreciated the way I used to carry the large slabs of meat on my shoulder, and they liked me. Yet I was slightly nervous that morning, heading over there not as one of Fleischer's workers but as my own boss, for the very first time.

The owner of the packing house, Milton Shloss, grabbed me and said, "I'm glad you left those people. They didn't treat you well." They had all heard the story. They knew I had asked for a raise and had been denied, and they knew that I had a sick child at home and that Fleischer had tried to prevent me from getting my papers from the Rabbi. He said, "You can take meat for three months without paying me."

Milton then called the foreman over and instructed him, "You give Boymel meat for three months and give him two cents less on the pound. He'll come in at 4 a.m. and pick up the meat himself."

There were twenty-five kosher butchers in Cincinnati. I was the twenty-sixth. I knew the business better than they did, and sold the meat at a low price. I already had a reduction of two cents off every pound courtesy of Milton Shloss, and I didn't need to make a big profit, not at first. But most importantly, I had the best meat. I went down personally in the morning and picked out the perfect slabs. Anybody who bought meat from me always said, "Mr. Boymel, no one has meat like yours."

I made my own corned beef and smoked meat and pastrami, spending long hours in the butcher shop basement. It was hard work, harder even than my days at Fleischer's butcher shop, but it was different: I was working for myself. It was my name on the front sign. Clients came in through word of mouth. I used to go to the synagogue and tell people I had a butcher's shop. That, combined with the quality of the meat, assured that our clientele grew from week to week.

Rachel worked in the butcher's shop with me. She cut meat, stood at the register and watched over the money. On the very first Friday of our first week in business, she put the cash in her pockets and went over to the packing house to pay them. They protested, "Mrs. Boymel, we told you that you didn't need to pay us for three months!" She replied calmly, "Mr. Shloss, it's not our money, and we won't spend it." We didn't need the money as long we had food and the store. We were in business.

The poor butcher's children

The American Jews looked down on us. No matter our accomplishments, they still thought of us as refugees. They used to call my son, Steve, "you poor butcher's son." They called my daughters "the poor butcher's daughters." It was the Jews, not the Gentiles, who were calling them these names.

My son and my older daughter would help out in the shop, delivering the meat. They were treated terribly. Our clients would not let them into their homes. My children were forced to leave the meat outside for them, and they wouldn't get paid.

I had an African-American worker who was very helpful. He was a good man. He took notice that there were some Jewish women who used to take meat for Shabbat and never pay. They'd come back in on Monday and say, "The meat was no good. I threw it out. I'm not going to pay for bad meat."

After that, the African-American worker, who was very smart, told one woman, "Please, don't throw the bad meat away. Bring it back and I'll go to the packing company and show them that they've sold us bad meat."

The woman said, "I'm not going to bring it back. I throw it straight in the garbage."

Of course, this wasn't true. She knew it, and he knew it as well. After that, she didn't show up at the store any more.

A working family

I worked very hard in the butcher's shop, rising in the early morning and coming home only in the late afternoon at the earliest. I told my husband Sam, "We have to have somebody watching the kids." Many other refugees were in our same situation, where both mother and father were forced to work long hours. Most of them simply gave their children a key to hang around their neck, and these children would return home alone to nothing but four walls. I didn't want that for my children. I was raised differently, and I was going to raise my children differently.

We found a babysitter and nanny to be home for our children. She told me she was eighteen years old, though I later found out that she was only sixteen when she started working for us. She stayed with our family until our youngest, Faye, was fifteen years old. She loved Faye as much as she would have loved her own child, treating Faye as her baby. She would even take her to her own house on occasion.

Steve helped us a lot, probably more than he should have. He knew that I needed all the help I could get, and he also knew that he was the eldest and that meant he needed to pitch in. I

depended on him. When I had a problem, I used to take him out
of school. I'd call on him to come and help me out with his sisters.
It hurts when I think about it now. I robbed him of his childhood.
He was a grown up boy before he got to be a child.

Luckily for me, Steve was a very understanding son. He
didn't hold anything against me. I recall how at student-parent
conferences I asked the teacher how Steve was doing, and she told
me she loved him, and more importantly – that she trusted him.
If it was very urgent to send a paper to another teacher, she could
count on Steve. She knew Steve wouldn't open it.

Patsy and Faye were born into a different reality than Steve's.
They could not remember the days when their father worked for
Fleischer and I worked as a babysitter. All they had ever known
was a family that had accomplished much and was on its way to
accomplishing even more. We were already in the "Golden Land,"
but had barely entered its gates. Within its confines they could
see other kids who were in a better state than they were, and it was
hard on them.

Sam and I had very little time for ourselves or for a social
life. We worked a six-day week, closing only on Saturday for the
Sabbath, but open on Sundays. On Saturday nights we had a
group of friends that used to get together and play cards. This get-
together took place just once a week because we had no more time
than that. Nevertheless, these were happy times. We were business
owners, and we were doing well for ourselves.

Menachem comes to America

Throughout the years I never abandoned my dream of bringing
my last remaining brother, Menachem, to be with me in America.
For a long while there was simply no way for me to achieve this,
not without being a citizen. Nevertheless, I began to look into it as
soon as Sam and I were settled. The people I worked with to bring
my brother over liked me so much, they promised that right after
I swore allegiance to the country, they would send my brother's

papers over. And they were true to their word. I swore allegiance in the morning, and I was awarded United States citizenship. My brother's papers were sent that afternoon.

My brother came alone. He and his family had already left Israel for Europe by then, and were all staying in Paris with other relatives. My brother's name was changed to Simon. A little later, his wife Edith joined him with their two children, Mazal and Pnina, who was named after my mother, too. Their third child was born in America. His name was Yankehl, after our father.

Simon had a "softer landing" in the United States than we did thanks to how far we had come. He stayed with us for a short while, and then I rented a place for him and his family. By the time his wife came he'd already furnished his apartment. We got him a job at Fleischer's as well, though it wasn't too long before we said, "That's enough with Fleischer. Come work with us."

In time he saved up enough money and bought himself a house across from where I lived, so our kids grew up together. They were either at my house or at his house. It was wonderful. They were very close, and both Simon and I were extremely thankful for this. Our family had been torn apart, but at least the next generation was given the chance to grow up together in peace, and to love and support each other.

THE NURSING HOME

"If you want your husband to live"

I owned and ran my butcher's shop, "Boymel Kosher Meats," for ten years. For the most part, I believed I had reached my final chapter; I had a healthy business and a healthy family, and I would continue to work and watch them grow up. But life had one more turn in store for me.

It first came in the unpleasant form of an ulcer. The meat business, it seemed, with its combination of constant worry and physically demanding work, was costing me my health. The pain and discomfort were sending me a message that was clear to me even before I'd visited the doctor, who told my wife in no uncertain terms, "Rachel, do you want your husband to live?"

Rachel exclaimed, "Of course I want him to live!"

The doctor nodded, expecting nothing less. He said, "If you want him to live, he has to get out of the butcher business."

But how were we to do that? It had taken me years of work, starting at Fleischer and leading up to our own butcher shop, to become my own man, a business owner with a loyal clientele and a steady income. The thought of having to start all over again, to reinvent myself at my age, was daunting.

138 Run, My Child

The auction

I had been mulling over the need for a new direction when a client entered my butcher's shop on a Friday morning and asked for some steaks. The man's name was Burt Bungolt, and if my ulcer was the first "visitor" informing me of the change to come, Burt was the second. He rifled through his wallet and said, "I don't have any money."

I said, "Take the steaks."

He nodded appreciatively and then, after giving this exchange a second thought, broke into speech. "You know, Sam, there is a nursing home that's going bankrupt." He said. "The owner has eight patients in the whole house, that's all. I work for the bank, you know, and the bank loaned this woman $120,000 for the nursing home, but she was driving with her lawyer boyfriend and they had an accident and she got killed. It was a tragedy. The bank had no choice but to take the loan away."

At this point I wasn't yet sure what Burt was trying to tell me. Was he simply making polite conversation as a way of showing friendly gratitude? Burt continued and said, "My point is, next week there's going to be an auction. Let's go to the auction. I'll take you."

All along my wife and I had been thinking we simply don't have the money to start a new business. We didn't believe that a bank would put faith in us, but Burt Bungolt was not only a banker, he was a man who knew us, and he trusted us. I understood immediately that he was offering me an opportunity I could not pass up.

Burt spoke to his boss on my behalf. I could hear Burt's side of the telephone conversation; he said, "Boymel is a very nice man. He owns a butcher shop, and he'll pay you." It felt good to be trusted like that.

Burt took me to the bank, where after a short introductory meeting with his boss he turned to me and said "It's settled, we'll go to the auction. We can bid up to $120,000, no more." The auction was a nail-biting affair for me. It seemed to be overflowing with bidders, and judging from their calm, collected manners, attending auctions was a matter of daily practice for them. They weren't bidding on their entire future the way I was.

Yet in a way, it was all very simple. I had only the potential loan of $120,000 to bid, no more, and so I did just that. I knew nothing about nursing homes, and I don't imagine that most people there did. It was the twenty five acres of land that were really for sale. Others bid $150,000 and up to $200,000. It was clear that we were not going to get it.

The auction was over. The highest bidders stepped up, paid their $30,000 down payment and were afforded thirty days to pay the rest of the sum off. As the winners walked out, one of the men said to me, quite offhandedly, "Give me $50,000, and I'll sell it to you." They were there to turn a quick profit. I left a bit dismayed, though I knew that I had done the right thing by turning him down. Opportunity had presented itself, and I had not remained passive. There was nothing more I could do.

Garden Manor

It was exactly thirty days later that I received the telephone call at the butcher's shop. It was Burt, and as he spoke I could hear the smile on his face. "Guess what?" he said, "The highest bidders couldn't come up with the money. They lost everything, all of their down payment. My boss said they're willing to give it to you for the $120,000, no auction, no bidding. They know you're good for it." And just like that, with one phone call, our lives changed.

After the Sabbath ended on Saturday night, I took my wife and we drove in the dark to survey our new land with our own eyes. I didn't know the way, and so we drove all night, getting lost and finding our way again, our spirits high and anxious. Now that it had suddenly been awarded to us, I had a burning need to see the place, to stand on our grounds. Finally, we found it. The sign read "Garden Manor."

We walked into the building and found it in a semi-decrepit state. Whoever had been running the place before us had not taken good care of it, that much was apparent. Rachel and I were not deterred; we knew it was the land that was important. I went over to the bank that Monday and signed the loan, officially owing them $120,000. The bank handed over a set of keys to me and said, "It's all yours."

My wife and I returned to see Garden Manor in the daylight. "My goodness," I said to myself. I believe Rachel's reaction was the same. The building seemed to be falling apart at the seams. There were eight patients there, barely clothed. There were two nurses in charge of their well-being. There was no toilet and there was no running water. There was no food. The people there, we learned, were paying $6 a day for this service.

My wife said, "You stay in the butcher's shop. I'll go here, to the nursing home. I'll run it."

She wasted no time. She turned to one of the nurses, a big woman, introduced herself and said, "Walk with me, please. Show me everything."

I believe the nurse was relieved to hear a strong voice in charge. She said, in a pleading voice, "There's no money here, and there's no food." Upon hearing that, my wife went out. She brought groceries, brought meat from our butcher shop, brought water and filled the nursing home with the smells of her cooking. The staff and the patients knew that day that things would never be the same at Garden Manor.

100% of the business

Though I knew enough about nursing homes to easily recognize Garden Manor's failings, by no means did I consider myself ready to run it. I had too much respect for the profession and for the patients who were in our care to believe that I could take over in a day. But I knew that I had the potential to learn and improve.

At first, my husband Sam opposed the idea of my working at the nursing home; he wanted me to be a housewife and spend time with the children. One of the first things he did was to hire a male nurse and sell him a 40% share of the business. This man was to take on the day-to-day responsibility of running the nursing home, and spare us the worry and pressure of running two businesses simultaneously.

One day my husband came home, placed a check firmly on the kitchen table and said, "Look at this check."

I looked at the check and immediately saw what had irked him. It was made out in my husband's name, but that was not my husband's signature at the bottom. The male nurse we'd put in charge was forging my husband's signature on checks.

I paid the nursing home a visit that week. It wasn't too early when I arrived, around 10 a.m., yet I found the male nurse sleeping on the job. There was a chauffer's apartment attached to the garage, which he had appropriated for his work-time naps. I knocked on the door repeatedly until the man finally awoke. He opened the door and eyed me groggily. I said, "What are you doing? Are you sleeping?" Ashamed, he hurriedly straightened up and got back on the job.

Continuing my impromptu inspections, I noticed on several occasions that when mail came in, he would toss out important papers and bills, and defer the payments until the last moment. I knew this much: this was not the way to run a business.

Other employees who had not been formally introduced to me began wondering who I was. The secretary said, "Excuse me, can I ask who you are?"

I said, "Yes. I am the boss's wife."

She said, "Oh. I thought that he was the boss." She gestured towards the male nurse.

"No, he works for us," I corrected her, intentionally leaving out the fact that he did indeed own 40% of the place. This was a situation that was making me increasingly uncomfortable.

To begin with, I called my lawyer and asked what I should do. I learned that I could have sued him; forging checks was an offense punishable by jail time. I wanted him out, but I didn't want to punish the man. All I wanted was to buy back his 40%. Armed with the knowledge that his offense had been severe, I confronted him. We had barely broached the subject, when the male nurse made it clear that he understood where things were headed.

He said, "Your husband is upset."

I told him, "Yes, he is upset. If I were you, I'd leave before he fires you."

"You know what," he said, "I'll listen to you."

That very week he came over to our house and gave up his 40% share. He signed it over to us, we refunded his initial sum in its entirety, and that was that. Garden Manor was again officially 100% our own.

The inspector

The next step was for me to learn the trade. But before I even had the chance to begin my learning process, I was visited by the state inspector who came in to inspect our nursing home. I had vaguely heard the name "Nurse McGoogan," along with whispers about her being a mean and strict inspector, but of course I didn't know what she looked like and I didn't recognize her when she stepped in. She began looking around inquisitively, but made no effort to introduce herself.

It was lunchtime when she arrived, and I was helping the staff carry the trays over to the tenants, so they could all receive their food while it was still hot. This had been one of the first changes we had implemented; we felt strongly that every tenant deserved a hot meal of quality food. I personally taught the staff how to cook, and the meat was provided by our butcher's shop – top quality.

The inspector stopped me on my way over to one of the tables. She peeked over into the tray and said, "Gee, this looks so good..."

I said, "My I ask you who you are?"

"Yes, I'm Miss McGoogan," she replied.

I said, "Would you mind waiting for one moment while I put this tray on the table? It's hot now, and I don't want them getting cold food."

She seemed a bit surprised, but she agreed. I believe that she was used to people treating her with caution or fear. When I returned to her, she inquired, "Who's cooking here? It smells so good."

I said, "It's my recipe. Come, eat."

Inspectors were not allowed to eat at the nursing homes they were evaluating, but Miss McGoogan couldn't help herself. She could tell that our food was special. Non-Jews simply don't cook like Jews. The style of the cooking and the flavoring were Jewish, and even though the food at the nursing home wasn't kosher, the meat was. Sam had shown the cooks how they were to soak the meat, so that when it was cut into there would be no blood.

As she ate, I decided that the only thing I could do was be upfront and honest with her. I said, "Miss McGoogan, I'm new to this. I don't know the nursing business yet. Can I ask one thing from you? If you have a problem, please don't write it in your book. Just tell me, and the next time you'll come, it will be fixed."

Miss McGoogan said, "You know what? I like you. You're a nice and honest woman. I can see that you're taking care of the people." She sat down with me and taught me what to do. I was getting priceless lessons for free, and I knew that I could do no wrong now. I had been taught by the inspector herself. Miss McGoogan loved the opportunity to share her knowledge with someone eager. She fell in love with me as well, and we remained the best of friends until she resigned. Even after I had learned all that she had to teach, we would get together for lunches.

The same approach worked just as well with the equipment inspector. His job was to perform periodic inspections to see if all the equipment was in order, checking if the refrigerator was sufficiently cold, if the air conditioning was working properly and the plumbing up to standards. I told him, "I need a favor from you."

He said, "What is it?"

"If you find something wrong, please don't write it in the book. Just give it to me in writing, and the next time you come here, it will be fixed."

This personal, honest approach, where I admitted that
I didn't know everything but demonstrated that I was willing to
learn, is what made me successful.

Eight times eight

My husband Sam stayed in the butcher business for that first year,
and I devoted the bulk of my time to running our nursing home.
As a businesswoman, I knew that in order to flourish, we needed
more tenants; eight simply were not enough.

I found the solution to this problem at a nearby psychiatric
hospital. The hospital housed those who couldn't afford other
arrangements. I could tell right away that most of the tenants
were not mentally ill. The criteria for their hospitalization
seemed to be quite lax; if they hadn't spoken at first or perhaps
were unable to speak English, the government threw them in
there.

I took a car, brought it up to the hospital and loaded in as
many patients at a time as I could and moved them to our home.
I was never afraid of them; contrary to the stigma of their illness,
they were all nice people. All they asked for was to be taken care
of, and they were perfectly pleasant. Their stay was government-
funded, and their quality of life improved drastically with the
move to Garden Manor.

Our nursing home was fixed up to house sixty-four patients
in preparation for the new arrivals. We had started out with merely
eight, and now we housed eight times that many.

I had prepared forty rooms, but faced with sixty-four
patients I was forced to come up with temporary solutions. The
chauffeur's quarters were converted into more space for tenants.
It was a beautiful apartment. For a while I was paid for sixty-four
people, mostly by the government, though I was only licensed for
forty. The inspector was aware of this but said nothing; it was clear
that although we had gone over our licensed limit, the tenants
were very well off.

Into the bank

Business was progressing nicely at the nursing home, but we had not yet reached the profits needed to fully repay the initial bank loan. Burt Bungolt's boss at the bank was a very nice and patient man who didn't apply any pressure on us to return the money quickly. Meanwhile, I understood that the only way to grow was to expand. Forty rooms just weren't going to be sufficient anymore, so I decided to build 140 new beds, meaning 140 new rooms.

Mr. Mondor, formerly of the IGA store, the same man who years earlier had helped me get my first business venture off the ground, proved himself to be invaluable, once again. He took it upon himself to introduce me to another bank, where he vouched for me. He said, "Look, I'll take it over. I know the president of this bank very well, and I'll tell him you're nice kids and you can run a nice nursing home."

The bank sent no fewer than six people over to the nursing home to inspect the way we were running it. We stood back quietly and let them study our system. Afterwards, I presented them with sketches of what I had planned for the place. They asked, "How can you do this? Do you have an architect?"

I replied, "Yes, I have an architect. What I need is $300,000 to build 140 new rooms."

They gave the plans another close inspection. They told me, "That's right, that's what you need." They left, taking our plans with them. Their demeanor revealed no clue as to what answer they were going to have for us.

The call came in to the butcher's shop. "Sam, grab a chair," the voice said. "I don't want you to fall down. We've gone over your case. We can see you're hard-working people. We can see you will do well. We saw what you did with your butcher shop, and you did a good job there. We just approved your $300,000. You can come and sign the papers with your wife, and the money's yours."

Rather than fall down, as the bank manager had feared I would, I sprang up in the air and ran out of the shop. Rachel and I rushed over to the bank. I parked in front of the bank window, bolted out of the car and through the bank door. My hand shook as I signed the loan papers. I couldn't believe it was actually happening.

When I walked out, the light of day was blinding for a moment. My wife walked beside me, and the lawyer who had overseen the signing walked by my other side. He was Greek, but he spoke Yiddish to me, asking me, "You know how lucky you are? Fifty people applied for the $300,000, and you were the one who got it. You better not fall down these stairs! You better hold on!"

I made it down the stairs without incident, but when I started the car, instead of pressing my foot to the brakes, I pressed the gas pedal. The car shot directly into the bank. Its glass wall shattered and shards rained across the hood of my car. Men scattered away from the point of collision, which sent a heavy desk careening into a chair.

Fortunately, no one was hurt. I sat behind the wheel, in shock. The bank officials hurried over to me and said, "Don't worry, we're not going to hurt you."

Of course, we had to pay for the damages done to the bank's exterior, but thanks to that very bank, we had the money to do so. And there was still plenty left over for the next big phase in our expansion. We began to build 140 new rooms…

My mother's voice

It didn't happen overnight, but by way of a lot of hard work we achieved more than we could have ever hoped for. Our dreams often scared us. Rachel used to sit and cry, "How are we going to do it? How are we going to pay the bank?" Yet even as she cried, she had faith. Rachel and I believed in God.

I used to hold conversations with my mother. Her memory was my strength. Her support and advice helped me at every turning point in my life. I said to her, "Mama, guide me. What should I do? I want to open another nursing home." I listened to her and opened another one. People around me were doubtful that it could succeed. They asked, "He's really opening another nursing home?" Today, we have six.

My mother's voice was alive inside of me. She said, "Don't

forget to give to charity and poor people." The first donations I was fortunate enough to make were to the Chabad House and the Yavneh Day School. I didn't have a lot of money back then, and though we were still abiding by our philosophy of saving for the future, we knew this did not exclude us from sharing what we did have.

My wife was charitable as well. She had learned this lesson from her mother, just as I had learned it from mine. Rachel told me how her mother's words had stayed with her: "If anybody comes and holds out a hand asking for charity, never let them go without." She used to deliver about $5,000 worth of meat from our butcher shop to poor people on Passover. Many cried and asked, "Mrs. Boymel, thank you! Why did you do this?"

My wife replied, "I didn't do it. God did it." She was not allowed to say that she did it.

As we found prosperity, I immediately created a foundation to ensure that part of the money would go to charity, toward the poor and toward the welfare of Israel. It brought me great joy to be able to provide for my family. I handed the butcher shop over to my brother-in-law Simon. My daughters were both married, and I took in my new sons-in-law and made them a part of our growing nursing home business, along with Steve, who had been there from the start.

I never talked about the Holocaust with anybody. I didn't think about it. My mind was on trying to build a business. We refugees would sometimes sit and talk amongst ourselves. On Saturdays we used to go to the park with our babies and talk. My mother's voice echoed within me, pleading me to tell the story. It would take me a long while before I could do what she asked.

We never talked about it

Sam and I never talked about the Holocaust. For years, no one wanted to hear about it. But as time passed, and the world began to understand the magnitude of what had transpired, stories like ours became sought after.

One of our employees at the nursing home was a dietician.

Her job was to write up the menus in accordance with state laws, as well as to know what substitutes were acceptable in case of certain shortages. I had been abiding by these laws before we'd brought her on, but it was required by law that we had a dietician on staff. I'm not sure how she learned of our past, but she approached me one day with a request. She wanted my husband to talk at her church about the Holocaust.

I had never been in a church before. Even when I visited Israel, I never set foot in a mosque or a church. But I couldn't disappoint my husband, so I went. As he spoke, I found I was shaking. His words took me back. After his speech, the congregation spoke to me as well, and I explained whatever I could. They thanked me, and afterwards the dietician took us out to a restaurant. In those days, I never ate in restaurants. It was an extremely emotional day for the both of us.

One day, when my son Steve was still a little boy, he asked "Mom, how come we don't have a grandma and a grandpa?"

I said, "Son, when you grow up a little bit, if you want to know, I'll tell you. I can't talk now."

Later, he heard me speak at all kinds of affairs. That day in the church was but the first time Sam or I would speak to an audience about our experiences. My children often attended these affairs. Other times, I spoke to them directly, though somehow that was much harder for me. Parts of my story came to them from other people. They had enough information to piece together my story and Sam's story.

They knew that I had survived with God's help, that He had sent angels to protect me. He had a reason that He wanted me to live. I was in danger of being killed so many times, and yet here I am. I have so many reasons to be thankful.

The "Bonds"

David Ben-Gurion, Israel's first Prime Minister, came to the United States in 1950 to launch the State of Israel Bonds. The idea to float bonds issued by Israel's government was Ben-Gurion's idea as a response to the economic devastation in the aftermath of Israel's War of Independence. At first, the Bonds were relatively unknown. I learned of them at a hotel in Chicago. A lot of people came to hear Ben-Gurion speak there. That speech was the first I had heard of the Bonds, and the first time I gave money, but hardly the last.

Back in Cincinnati I took it upon myself to convince fellow Jews to invest in Israel Bonds. It helped that "the Bonds" had a very good name. To this day, Israel has never defaulted on payment of principal, interest, or maturity amount on any of the securities it has issued. I belonged to a country club in Cincinnati, and I would regularly meet Jewish men there. I'd say, for example, "I'm buying for $200,000. Yankeh, do you want to buy for $200,000?" And Yankeh would say, "Sam, I can't say no to you."

In return, the Israel Bonds organization honored me several times in different cities in the United States. I stood up and spoke, and though my English was far from perfect, and I often employed Yiddish when at a loss, my words touched my listeners' hearts. I spoke openly and honestly about what had happened to the Jews and about what I had experienced firsthand. After each of my accounts, people came up to me and said to me, "Sam, when you speak, we sell a lot of Bonds." I finally felt that I was fulfilling my mother's wishes.

Turzysk

My work with the Bonds brought me to Israel many times. I became acquainted with people from my hometown of Turzysk who had made a life for themselves in Israel. I would often invite them to meet me. One of these men, Ben Zion Weiner, was devoted to the memory of Turzysk. He built a model of the lost *shtetl* that was on display in Israel.

Ben Zion called me and told me, "Sam, I went to Turzysk. You can see all the bones there from the mass grave. You should see the cows and the pigs eating those bones. It's a terrible sight."

He wanted my help to build a respectable monument worthy of the memory of all who had lost their lives in Turzysk. I became involved, directed Ben Zion to the people I believed would do a proper job, and supplied the funds. I also sponsored the return trips of other Turzysk men and women who wanted to revisit their pasts. However, it was a while before I mustered the strength to do so myself.

The bones in the shtetl

My son Steve had expressed his wish to see Turzysk many times. He finally got through to me in the year 2000. He said, "Dad, you're getting old. You're in your seventies. Let's go there. I want to see where you came from, and how you survived." The other children didn't want to do it; they didn't believe in going. But Steve convinced us. My wife Rachel and I went along with Steve, her brother Simon and about twenty people from Israel.

We arrived in Warsaw and traveled by bus to Turzysk. Even though nearly sixty years had passed, once I stepped on the soil of my past I felt as if it had just happened. I couldn't take it; the emotions were overwhelming. As we neared the monument, we met several old Poles. They were very nice to us, but they sent chills down my spine when they said they remembered me and my family walking to the grave.

The monument had already been erected by the time we came to Turzysk, and it was beautiful. I walked over to the graves and I spoke to my mother. I had carried her with me everywhere I'd gone in life, and I'd spoken to her often, but standing in the place of her death was a different experience altogether. Tears streamed down my cheeks. I said to my wife and son, "I want to go back to the hotel, I can't take it. It's too much for me."

We remained in Turzysk for five days. I learned that although the monument had been built, bringing the bones to proper burial had proven too difficult due to large accumulations of water. I walked around and saw many bones that had been brought to the surface in pools of undrained water. My son had invited a doctor from Warsaw to join our group. Upon seeing the bones, the doctor started crying. He said, "Those are the bones of the Jewish people."

I couldn't bear the sight of these abandoned remains. I knew that the bones could have been anyone's; they could have been my mother's.

After some organization, I finally found a way to bring them to a fitting Jewish burial. I said the Kaddish. I spoke with great emotion about what my family and the entire Jewish population of Turzysk had gone through, and the great significance this day held for me. Steve spoke of his feelings as well. The skies rained on us.

AFTERWORD

Sam and Rachel, A Life of Accomplishment

Rachel Boymel lives by the code, "Nothing has made us feel more fortunate than to have had the means to help others." She has been involved in numerous projects in Israel, such as the Boymel Tennis Center, Nahariya, as well as in the US, helping to establish Jewish schools in Cincinnati. Her only wish for the future is peace for Israel.

Sam is proud to be involved in charities as well as his own business: "Still," he says, "I consider myself a plain guy." His definition of joy is, "as long as you have something to eat, as long as you can feed your family, you're a happy man." However, he adds, "when I go to bed I think about my parents. The pain remains real. Whatever I did in my lifetime, I did for them...." Writing his memoirs and being involved in the creation of the United States Holocaust Memorial Museum in Washington DC are part of Sam's lifelong mission to perpetuate the memory of the Holocaust.

Nevertheless, Sam and Rachel have their eyes not only on the past but also on the future, dedicating contributions to educational institutions in Israel such as Yad Labanim in Nahariya, Project Renewal, an Ethiopian community center, as well as sponsoring

Israeli children at an American summer camp. They have generously supported the construction of hospital wings, synagogues, Jewish community centers, schools, and especially the Israel Bonds Campaign, Friends of Israel, Beit Halochem and more. The Boymels have met with numerous distinguished leaders in the US and in Israel.

Yad Vashem wishes Rachel and Sam Boymel "*Ad 120*," good health and continued happiness until the age of one hundred and twenty. Sam Boymel has indeed honored the memory of his beloved mother and perpetuated the memory of the Jews of his hometown, the vanished Jewish community of Turzysk.

Sam's mother would have been extremely proud.

Shraga I. Mekel
American Society for Yad Vashem

Rachel and Sam, 1945

Rachel and Sam, after the war

Early photos of Sam and Rachel's children: Steve (bottom),
Patsy (top right) and Faye (top left)

Sam and Rachel with their children Steve (center) and Patsy, Cincinnati, c. 1950

The Boymel family, c. 1983. Left to right: Faye, Rachel, Sam, Patsy, Steve

Sam with Prime Minister Yitzhak Rabin (left), 1976

Sam and Rachel with their children and grandchildren, 1988

Sam and Rachel at the Boymel Tennis Center, Nahariya, Israel, 1990

Sam with General Colin Powell (center) and CEO and Chairman of US
Bancorp Jerry Grundhofer, 1994

Sam and Rachel with Henry Kissinger, 1995

Sam and Rachel with Hillary Rodham Clinton (center), 2002

Rachel and Sam, 1995